THE AUSTRALIAN

Women's Weekly

Christmas

contents

Party food & drinks

Plan the number of different foods and drinks you need based on what time of day they are to be served, the number of guests, and what food will follow. If the food and drinks are preceding a main meal, you only need to sharpen your guests' appetites (less is best) so two different foods (allow four morsels per person) and drinks will be enough. If you're just serving finger food with drinks, allow at least 12 single servings of food per person.

zucchini and corn fritters with crème fraîche

½ cup (75g) plain flour
½ cup (75g) self-raising flour
2 eggs
½ cup (140g) yogurt
½ teaspoon caster sugar
420g can corn kernels, drained
2 small zucchini (180g), grated coarsely
2 cloves garlic, crushed
1 small red onion (100g), chopped finely
2 tablespoons finely chopped fresh basil
1 tablespoon finely chopped fresh
    tarragon
¼ cup (20g) finely grated
    parmesan cheese
2 tablespoons olive oil
¾ cup (180g) crème fraîche
⅓ cup (50g) pine nuts, roasted
⅓ cup fresh baby basil leaves

1 Combine flours in large bowl; whisk in eggs, yogurt and sugar. Stir in corn, zucchini, garlic, onion, chopped herbs and cheese; stand 15 minutes.
2 Heat oil in large frying pan; cook heaped teaspoons of mixture, in batches, until browned both sides. Cool on wire racks.
3 Serve fritters topped with crème fraîche, pine nuts and basil leaves.

----

prep + cook time 40 minutes (+ standing) makes 50

Fresh corn can be used instead of canned corn; you will need 2 cobs.
Sour cream or yogurt can be used instead of the crème fraîche.
Fritters can be made the day before; top them with crème fraîche etc, an hour or so before serving.

campari sorbet sparkler

Combine 1⅓ cups caster sugar, 1 cup grapefruit juice and 2 tablespoons glucose syrup in small saucepan; bring to the boil. Stir over medium heat until sugar dissolves; cool. Stir in ¼ cup lemon juice, 2 cups grapefruit juice and 60ml Campari. Churn in an ice-cream maker, according to manufacturer's instructions; freeze for 4 hours. Serve scoops of sorbet in cocktail glasses topped with Champagne or sparkling white wine.

prep + cook time 20 minutes
(+ churning and freezing) **serves** 16

papaya and orange spritzer

Peel, seed and coarsely chop 1 small papaya. Blend or process papaya with 1 cup orange juice and ¾ cup coconut-flavoured liqueur until smooth. Place ice-cubes and a few mint leaves in eight tall glasses. Divide papaya mixture between glasses; top up glasses with 1 litre chilled sweet apple cider.

prep time 10 minutes **serves** 8 (makes 1 litre)

lime and mango tropicana

Combine strained pulp from 4 passionfruit and flesh from
2 medium ripe mangoes in blender; blend until smooth.
Combine ½ cup lime juice, 4 cups lemonade and ⅔ cup
citrus-flavoured liqueur (such as Cointreau) in large jug; stir
in mango mixture. Serve over ice in tall glasses.

prep time 15 minutes   **serves** 8 (makes 2 litres)

sparkling burgundy and cranberry punch

Combine 1¼ cups cranberry juice and 1 cup white sugar in small
saucepan; stir over heat until sugar dissolves. Bring to the boil;
remove from heat. Add 1 black-leaf tea bag, stand 15 minutes;
discard tea bag, cool tea. Combine 125g raspberries, 250g hulled
and quartered strawberries and 125g blueberries in a large jug.
Stir in 2 cups ice-cubes and cranberry mixture; refrigerate 2 hours.
Stir in 750ml bottle sparkling burgundy before serving.

prep + cook time 15 minutes
(+ standing and refrigeration) **serves** 8 (makes 2 litres)

You can buy cooked crab meat at the local fish markets or supermarket. Alternatively, buy fresh crabs and cook them (blue swimmer crabs are good). To tell if crabs are meaty, look at the claws; if they are pointy and sharp it means they have a new shell and don't have much meat. If the claws are rounded, they have an older shell and will have more meat.

green onion blinis with chilli crab salad

⅔ cup (100g) wholemeal plain flour
¼ cup (35g) white self-raising flour
1 tablespoon plain flour
½ teaspoon cayenne pepper
2 eggs
¾ cup (180ml) buttermilk
2 green onions, sliced finely
40g butter, melted
chilli crab salad
150g cooked crab meat
1 tablespoon finely chopped fresh mint
1 tablespoon finely chopped fresh vietnamese mint
1 teaspoon finely grated lime rind
2 tablespoons lime juice
2 teaspoons fish sauce
½ lebanese cucumber (65g), seeded, chopped finely
1 fresh small red thai chilli, sliced thinly

1 Sift flours and pepper into medium bowl; whisk in eggs and buttermilk until smooth. Stir in onion and butter.
2 Heat oiled large frying pan; cook level tablespoons of blini mixture, in batches, until golden both sides. Cool on wire racks.
3 Meanwhile, make chilli crab salad.
4 Serve blinis topped with salad.
chilli crab salad Combine ingredients in medium bowl; season to taste.

prep + cook time 40 minutes (+ cooling) **makes** 24

You could serve the crab mixture on mini toasts, lavash or sliced french bread stick.

lamb cutlets with sumac yogurt

2 tablespoons za'atar
¼ cup (60ml) olive oil
1 tablespoon dried oregano
2 cloves garlic, crushed
2 teaspoons finely grated lemon rind
2 tablespoons lemon juice
24 french-trimmed lamb cutlets (1.2kg)
48 small fresh mint leaves
sumac yogurt
1 cup (280g) yogurt
1 clove garlic, crushed
1 lebanese cucumber (130g), seeded, chopped finely
2 teaspoons sumac

1   Combine za'atar, oil, oregano, garlic, rind and juice in large bowl; add lamb, turn to coat in mixture. Cover; refrigerate 3 hours or overnight.
2   Make sumac yogurt.
3   Cook cutlets, in batches, on heated oiled barbecue (or grill or grill plate). Serve cutlets warm topped with sumac yogurt and 2 mint leaves each.
sumac yogurt   Combine ingredients in small bowl; season to taste.

prep + cook time 30 minutes (+ refrigeration) makes 24

Lamb can be marinated and sumac yogurt made a day ahead; keep, covered, in the refrigerator. Za'atar is a Middle-Eastern herb and spice mix made with sumac, thyme, roasted sesame seeds, marjoram, oregano and sea salt; it is available from spice shops, Middle-Eastern food shops and delicatessens. A moroccan spice blend, available from supermarkets, can be used instead.

skewered prawns with chilli marinade

24 uncooked medium king prawns (1kg)
3 limes
1 tablespoon peanut oil
2 fresh kaffir lime leaves, shredded finely
0.5cm piece fresh ginger (2.5g), grated
2 teaspoons sambal oelek
1 teaspoon sesame oil
2 tablespoons japanese soy sauce
2 tablespoons mirin

1 Shell and devein prawns leaving tails intact. Quarter limes lengthways; cut each quarter in half lengthways to give a total of 24 wedges. Thread prawns onto skewers; followed by a lime wedge.
2 Combine remaining ingredients in small bowl; season to taste. Brush skewers with half the marinade. Cover, refrigerate 1 hour.
3 Cook skewers, in batches, on heated oiled grill plate (or grill or barbecue), until prawns are browned, brushing with remaining marinade occasionally. Serve immediately.

prep + cook time 30 minutes (+ refrigeration)
makes 24

You need 24 bamboo skewers for this recipe; soak them in cold water for at least an hour before using to prevent scorching during cooking.

smoked chicken crostini

1½ cups (180g) shredded smoked chicken
2 shallots (50g), chopped finely
¼ cup (30g) finely chopped celery
¼ cup (25g) walnuts, roasted, chopped coarsely
1 tablespoon finely chopped fresh tarragon
¼ cup (75g) mayonnaise
1 teaspoon wholegrain mustard
1 tablespoon preserved lemon rind, chopped finely
1 small french bread stick (150g), cut into 24 slices
1 large clove garlic, halved
2 tablespoons olive oil
1 small pear (180g), cut into matchsticks

1 Combine chicken, shallot, celery, nuts, tarragon, mayonnaise, mustard and preserved lemon in medium bowl; season to taste.
2 Toast bread slices, in batches, on heated grill plate (or grill or barbecue). Rub one side with garlic, brush with oil; season to taste.
3 Serve crostini topped with chicken mixture and pear.

----

prep + cook time 30 minutes **makes** 24

You need to buy about 250g smoked chicken breast for this recipe. Chicken mixture can be prepared a day ahead; keep, covered, in the refrigerator.
Preserved lemons can be bought from delis and some supermarkets. Remove a piece of lemon from the jar, discard the lemon flesh. Rinse the rind under water, dry, then chop finely.

prawns with basil remoulade

48 cooked medium king prawns (2kg)
basil remoulade
1 tablespoon olive oil
1 small leek (200g), sliced thinly
½ cup coarsely chopped fresh basil leaves
¼ cup coarsely chopped fresh flat-leaf parsley leaves
2 tablespoons coarsely chopped cornichons
2 egg yolks
2 teaspoons white wine vinegar
2 teaspoons dijon mustard
1 cup (250ml) vegetable oil
1 tablespoon lemon juice
2 teaspoons warm water

1   Shell and devein prawns leaving tails intact.
2   Make basil remoulade.
3   Serve prawns with remoulade.

basil remoulade Heat olive oil in small saucepan; cook leek, covered, over low heat, about 10 minutes or until soft, cool. Blend or process basil, parsley, cornichons, egg yolks, vinegar and mustard until smooth. With motor operating, gradually add vegetable oil in a thin steady stream; blend until thick. Stir in juice and the water, then leeks; season to taste.

----

prep + cook time 30 minutes serves 8

Use a bland tasting vegetable oil or a light olive oil for the remoulade; it can be made a day ahead and kept, covered, in the fridge.

Use a soft creamy blue cheese for the blue cheese mousse; the mousse can be made a day ahead and kept, covered, in the fridge. It's best to cook the beef as close to serving time as possible.

peppered beef with blue cheese mousse

500g beef fillet, trimmed
¼ cup (60ml) olive oil
2 tablespoons finely cracked black pepper
180g packet lavash crispbreads
1 small bunch watercress
blue cheese mousse
100g blue cheese, softened
100g packaged cream cheese, softened
⅓ cup (60ml) cream

1 Halve beef lengthways; rub with oil and pepper. Cook beef on heated oiled grill plate (or grill or barbecue) until cooked to your liking, turning beef once. Cover beef; stand 10 minutes before slicing thinly.
2 Meanwhile, make blue cheese mousse.
3 Serve lavash topped with beef, some of the mousse, and sprigs of watercress.
blue cheese mousse Stir ingredients together until smooth. Season to taste.

prep + cook time 30 minutes **makes** 48

For an earthier flavour, barbecue the whole eggplant. First prick the skin all over with a fork, then cook the eggplant for about 30 minutes – depending on its size and the heat of the barbecue – or until the eggplant collapses. Cool the eggplant, peel away the skin, then proceed with the recipe.

spiced eggplant and haloumi tarts

1 medium eggplant (300g), peeled, chopped coarsely
1 teaspoon ground cumin
1 teaspoon ground coriander
2 tablespoons olive oil
¼ cup (55g) finely packed brown sugar
¼ cup (60ml) water
¼ cup (60ml) lime juice (see note below)
2 tablespoons finely chopped fresh flat-leaf parsley
100g haloumi cheese, sliced thickly
2 tablespoons lemon juice
1 teaspoon finely cracked black pepper
30 baked mini shortcrust or puff pastry tart shells

1 Preheat oven to 200°C/180°C fan-forced.
2 Toss eggplant, cumin, coriander and oil in small baking dish; season. Cover dish; roast 20 minutes. Remove cover, roast 10 minutes or until eggplant is tender.
3 Combine sugar and the water in small saucepan; stir over heat until sugar dissolves.
4 Blend or process eggplant mixture, sugar syrup and lime juice until eggplant is coarsely chopped. Stir in parsley; cover to keep warm.
5 Sprinkle cheese with lemon juice and pepper; cook on heated barbecue (or grill or grill plate) until browned both sides. Chop cheese into 30 pieces.
6 Meanwhile, fill tart shells with warm eggplant mixture; top with cheese, and fine shreds of lime rind.

prep + cook time 50 minutes **makes** 30

Mini shortcrust and puff pastry tart shells are available from most major supermarkets and delicatessens. Shred thin strips of rind from lime to garnish tarts.

The big day

The key to making a success of the meal on the big day is all about planning and preparation. If you're not already a list-maker, become one; having a list will make everything seem so much easier. Prepare as much of the food ahead as possible, give reliable people jobs to do by a certain time, don't forget the children – before they get their presents would be best – they love to be involved. Make sure you plan to enjoy the big day, too.

lobster with asian-style slaw

2 cooked large lobsters (2.5kg)
1 small mango (300g), sliced thinly
1 small green mango (350g), grated finely
½ cup loosely packed fresh thai basil leaves
½ cup loosely packed fresh coriander leaves
½ cup loosely packed fresh mint leaves
1 cup (80g) finely shredded red cabbage
1 cup (80g) finely shredded wombok
wasabi and coconut dressing
¾ cup (225g) mayonnaise
¼ cup (60ml) coconut cream
2 teaspoons finely grated lime rind
2 tablespoons lime juice
2 tablespoons mirin
1 teaspoon wasabi paste

1 Make wasabi and coconut dressing.
2 Remove head from lobster; using kitchen scissors cut away shell, remove flesh. Slice lobster thickly crossways. Combine in medium bowl with two-thirds of the dressing.
3 Combine mango and remaining ingredients in medium bowl, season to taste. Divide lobster and slaw between serving plates; serve drizzled with remaining dressing.
wasabi and coconut dressing Whisk ingredients in small bowl; season to taste.

----

prep + cook time 45 minutes **serves** 8

Green papaya can be used instead of green mango. Both are available from Asian greengrocers and some larger supermarkets.
Thai basil is available from Asian greengrocers and most major supermarkets; you can use regular basil if thai basil is not available.

prawn cocktail

1kg cooked medium king prawns
⅓ cup (100g) mayonnaise
2 tablespoons cream
1 tablespoon tomato sauce
1 teaspoon worcestershire sauce
½ teaspoon Tabasco sauce
½ teaspoon dijon mustard
2 teaspoons lemon juice
8 baby cos lettuce leaves

1   Shell and devein prawns.
2   Combine mayonnaise, cream, sauces, mustard and juice in small bowl; season to taste.
3   Divide lettuce between four glasses; top with prawns, drizzle with sauce. Serve with lemon wedges.

----

prep time 30 minutes **serves** 4

Use a good quality egg-based mayonnaise for this recipe.

melon in prosciutto

1 small rockmelon (1.3kg), halved lengthways
12 slices prosciutto (180g)
2 tablespoons olive oil
¼ cup loosely packed fresh flat-leaf parsley leaves

1   Peel and seed rockmelon; cut into 12 wedges.
2   Wrap prosciutto around melon wedges; drizzle with oil, then sprinkle with parsley.

----

prep time 15 minutes **serves** 4

Use a good quality extra virgin olive oil for the best flavour.

goats cheese gateau

½ cup (140g) bottled roasted red capsicum, drained
250g packet cream cheese, softened
2 tablespoons lemon juice
360g goats cheese, softened
¼ cup (60ml) cream
1 tablespoon finely chopped preserved lemon rind
2 teaspoons finely grated lemon rind
2 tablespoons finely chopped fresh chervil
bagel crisps and salad leaves, to serve
grape juice glaze
¾ cup (180ml) grape juice
2 teaspoons gelatine
1 tablespoon caster sugar
¼ cup (60ml) port

1   Grease 20cm springform tin, line base and side with baking paper.
2   Blend or process capsicum, cream cheese and 1 tablespoon of the juice until combined; season to taste. Spread into tin, cover; refrigerate 30 minutes.
3   Blend or process goats cheese, cream, preserved lemon, lemon rind, chervil and remaining juice until combined; season to taste. Spread evenly over capsicum mixture, cover; refrigerate 30 minutes.
4   Meanwhile, make grape juice glaze; cool. Pour glaze over cheese mixture. Cover; refrigerate overnight.
5   Remove gateau from pan; serve cold with bagel crisps and salad leaves.
grape juice glaze Place ¼ cup of the grape juice in small heatproof jug in pan of simmering water, add gelatine; stir until dissolved, cool. Combine remaining grape juice and sugar in small saucepan; stir over low heat until sugar dissolves, cool. Stir in port and gelatine mixture.

prep + cook time 1 hour (+ refrigeration and cooling)
serves 16

Preserved lemons can be bought from delis and some supermarkets. Remove a piece of lemon from the jar, discard the lemon flesh. Rinse the rind under water, dry, then chop finely.

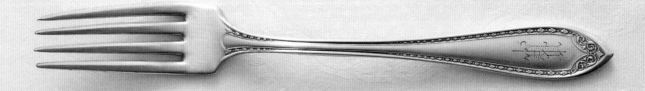

We used kingfish here, but you can use any firm white fish you like. Your fishmonger will advise you of the best fish to use for this recipe. Any sashimi quality fish will work well. Ask the fishmonger to slice the fish finely for you to save time. The fish will be "cooked" by the dressing.

fish with ginger and shallot dressing

1 medium pomegranate (320g)
480g piece kingfish, skin and bones removed
100g fetta cheese, cut into small cubes
2 tablespoons finely chopped fresh chives
fried shallots and lime wedges, to serve
ginger and shallot dressing
1 shallot (25g), chopped finely
1 tablespoon drained pickled pink ginger,
    chopped finely
1 teaspoon lime juice
2 teaspoons caster sugar
2 tablespoons japanese soy sauce
¼ cup (60ml) olive oil

1 Make ginger and shallot dressing.
2 Remove seeds from pomegranate; drain. You need ½ cup pomegranate seeds.
3 Slice fish thinly, place on serving plates. Top with cheese, chives and pomegranate seeds; drizzle with dressing, stand 5 minutes. Serve sprinkled with fried shallots, and lime segments.
ginger and shallot dressing Combine ingredients in screw-top jar; shake well, season to taste.

prep time 30 minutes **serves** 6

To remove pulp (seeds) from pomegranate, cut in half crossways. Hold one half over a bowl, firmly tap on the skin with a wooden spoon or rolling pin, the seeds should fall out into the bowl.
Fried shallots are available from Asian grocery stores, or you can gently fry thinly sliced shallots until crisp.

marinated duck with peppered strawberries

¾ cup (225g) rock salt
¾ cup (165g) firmly packed brown sugar
2 tablespoons sichuan pepper
4 x 220g duck breasts
70g baby rocket leaves
peppered strawberries
250g strawberries, hulled, halved
½ teaspoon ground white pepper
½ teaspoon finely cracked black pepper
¼ cup (60ml) olive oil
1½ cups (225g) cherries, seeded, halved
2 tablespoons balsamic vinegar
1 tablespoon finely grated orange rind
2 tablespoons orange juice
2 shallots (50g) chopped finely

1   Combine rock salt, sugar and pepper in large bowl, add duck breasts; turn to coat. Cover; refrigerate 3 hours.
2   Brush off marinade; pat duck dry with absorbent paper. Place duck, skin-side down, in lightly oiled heated large frying pan; cook, over low heat, about 20 minutes or until skin is browned. Turn duck; cook about 4 minutes or until cooked to your liking. Remove duck from pan, cover loosely with foil; stand 10 minutes before slicing thickly.
3   Meanwhile, make peppered strawberries.
4   Serve rocket with strawberries and duck.
peppered strawberries Combine berries, peppers and 1 tablespoon of the oil in medium bowl. Cook strawberry mixture on hot grill plate (or barbecue) for 30 seconds. Transfer to medium bowl; cool. Stir in cherries, vinegar, rind, juice, shallot and remaining oil.

prep + cook time 45 minutes (+ refrigeration)
serves 6

Duck breasts are available from poultry shops and some butcher shops.

smoked salmon with capers

320g sliced smoked salmon
1 small red onion (100g), chopped finely
½ cup (90g) rinsed, drained baby capers
2 small witlof (110g), leaves separated
1 baby fennel bulb (130g), sliced thinly
2 red radishes (70g), trimmed, sliced thinly
mustard honey dressing
1 teaspoon dijon mustard
2 teaspoons honey
2 tablespoons lemon juice
1 tablespoon finely chopped fresh dill
¼ cup (60ml) olive oil

1 Make mustard honey dressing.
2 Divide salmon between serving plates; sprinkle with onion and capers. Serve with witlof, fennel and radish; drizzle with dressing.
mustard honey dressing Combine ingredients in screw-top jar; shake well. Season to taste.

prep + cook time 25 minutes **serves** 8

A charcuterie plate consists of cured or prepared meats (most often pork). To save time, purchase various preserves and dips from the supermarket, instead of making the pickled mushrooms and carrot salad. Water crackers and oat cakes can be served instead of the sourdough.

charcuterie plate

1 tablespoon finely chopped fresh tarragon
2 tablespoons olive oil
24 cherry tomatoes (250g)
1 loaf sourdough bread (675g), sliced thickly
150g thinly sliced prosciutto
150g thinly sliced salami
150g thinly sliced pastrami
120g chicken liver pâté
pickled mushrooms
2 tablespoons olive oil
50g shiitake mushrooms, trimmed
70g swiss brown mushrooms, quartered
100g enoki mushrooms, trimmed
3 fresh small red thai chillies
4 sprigs fresh thyme
1 tablespoon caster sugar
2 tablespoons sherry vinegar
carrot and turmeric salad
1 large carrot (180g), cut into matchsticks
¾ cup (225g) mayonnaise
2 teaspoons finely grated lime rind
2 teaspoons lime juice
1 teaspoon ground turmeric
1 teaspoon yellow mustard seeds, toasted
2 tablespoons finely chopped fresh chives

1 Make pickled mushrooms; make carrot and turmeric salad.
2 Combine tarragon and oil in medium bowl; season to taste. Add tomatoes; mix gently.
3 Char-grill or toast sourdough.
4 Serve tomato mixture, sliced meats, pâté and toasts with mushrooms and salad.
pickled mushrooms Heat oil in large frying pan, add mushrooms, chillies and thyme; stir over medium heat 1 minute. Stir in sugar then vinegar; stir until mushrooms are tender. Cool, season to taste.
carrot and turmeric salad Combine ingredients in medium bowl; season to taste.

prep + cook time 45 minutes **serves** 10

We used pacific oysters in this recipe, because their full-bodied flavour teams well with these robust dressings.

oysters with three toppings

36 oysters (900g), on the half shell
coarse rock salt
ponzu dressing
2 tablespoons light soy sauce
2 teaspoons peanut oil
2 teaspoons mirin
1 tablespoon brown sugar
2 tablespoons lime juice
shallot dressing
⅓ cup (80ml) white wine vinegar
3 shallots (75g), chopped finely
green mango and cucumber salsa
½ lebanese cucumber (65g), seeded, chopped finely
1 tablespoon finely shredded green mango
1 tablespoon finely chopped red onion
1 teaspoon finely grated lime rind
1 teaspoon lime juice
1 teaspoon fish sauce
1 tablespoon vegetable oil

1 Make ponzu dressing, shallot dressing and green mango and cucumber salsa.
2 Serve oysters on bed of rock salt; serve dressings with oysters.
ponzu dressing Combine sauce, oil, mirin and sugar in medium saucepan; stir over low heat until sugar dissolves. Add juice; season to taste, cool.
shallot dressing Bring vinegar to the boil in small saucepan; remove from heat. Add shallot; cool.
green mango and cucumber salsa Combine ingredients in small bowl; season to taste.

prep + cook time 30 minutes (+ cooling) **serves** 6

The ponzu dressing will keep for up to two weeks in the refrigerator. The shallot dressing and the salsa are best made on the day of serving.
Instead of coarse rock salt, you can serve the oysters on a bed of crushed ice.

31

prawn and scallop tortellini

500g uncooked medium king prawns,
    shelled, deveined
250g scallops without roe
1 tablespoon olive oil
2 tablespoons finely chopped fresh vietnamese mint
2 tablespoons finely chopped fresh chervil
2 tablespoons finely chopped preserved lemon rind
2 teaspoons sea salt
1 teaspoon cracked black pepper
220g soft goats cheese
275g packet round gow gee wrappers
lemon dressing
¼ cup (60ml) lemon juice
½ cup (125ml) olive oil
1 tablespoon finely chopped fresh chervil
1 tablespoon finely chopped fresh flat-leaf parsley

1   Make lemon dressing.
2   Coarsely chop prawns and scallops. Heat oil in large frying pan; cook seafood over medium heat until prawns change colour, cool.
3   Combine seafood, herbs, preserved lemon, salt, pepper and goats cheese in medium bowl.
4   To make tortellini, place a gow gee wrapper on bench; place 1 level tablespoon of the seafood mixture in centre, brush edge with water. Fold in half; bring two points together to make a crescent shape, press gently to seal. Repeat with remaining ingredients.
5   Cook tortellini in large saucepan of boiling water until tortellini floats to the top; drain. Transfer tortellini to large heatproof bowl; drizzle with a little dressing.
6   Serve tortellini drizzled with remaining dressing; sprinkle with extra chervil sprigs to serve.
lemon dressing Combine ingredients in screw-top jar; shake well. Season to taste.

prep + cook time 40 minutes **serves** 6

Cover gow gees with a damp tea towel to stop them drying out while making the tortellini. The tortellini can be made a day ahead; store, in a single layer, covered in plastic wrap, in the refrigerator until ready to cook.
Preserved lemons can be bought from delis and some supermarkets. Remove a piece of lemon from the jar, discard the lemon flesh. Rinse the rind under water, dry, then chop finely.

smoked trout and avocado salad with sour cream dressing

2 smoked rainbow trout (600g)
2 large avocados (640g), chopped coarsely
2 lebanese cucumbers (260g), cut into ribbons
6 bocconcini cheese (360g), drained, quartered
3 shallots (75g), sliced thinly
60g baby rocket leaves
sour cream dressing
10g baby rocket leaves
¾ cup (180g) sour cream
1 tablespoon finely grated lemon rind
2 tablespoons lemon juice
1 tablespoon olive oil

1   Make sour cream dressing.
2   Remove skin and bones from fish, flake into bite-size pieces. Combine fish, avocado, cucumber, cheese, shallot and rocket in large bowl; serve drizzled with dressing.
sour cream dressing Blend or process ingredients until combined; season to taste.

prep time 25 minutes **serves** 8

You can substitute salmon, tuna or swordfish for the trout.

fig, onion and bocconcini tart

2 tablespoons olive oil
2 large red onions (600g), sliced finely
1 tablespoon finely chopped fresh thyme
1 tablespoon finely grated lemon rind
2 tablespoons brown sugar
¼ cup (60ml) dry red wine
2 sheets puff pastry
1 egg, beaten lightly
10 fresh medium figs (600g), quartered
260g bocconcini cheese, drained, quartered
20g baby rocket leaves

1   Preheat oven to 220°C/200°C fan-forced.
2   Heat oil in large frying pan, add onion, thyme, rind and sugar; stir over medium heat, about 3 minutes or until onion is soft. Add wine; stir over low heat until wine has evaporated.
3   Line two oven trays with baking paper; place one pastry sheet on each. With the back of a knife, mark a 2cm border around edge of each pastry sheet; brush border with egg; refrigerate 10 minutes.
4   Spread onion mixture over pastry sheets within borders; bake 10 minutes. Remove from oven; top with figs; bake about 10 minutes or until figs are browned.
5   Cut each tart into four; top with cheese and rocket, season to taste.

prep + cook time 45 minutes **serves** 8

Use figs that are not too ripe. Overripe figs contain more moisture and will make the pastry soggy.

The pork neck can be marinated in the glaze the day before. The pork and potatoes can be roasted in an oven at 180°C/160°C fan-forced. The potato salad can be served hot or cold.

spiced pork neck with potato salad

1 cup (250ml) water
¾ cup (165g) firmly packed brown sugar
2 fresh long red chillies, chopped finely
2 cloves garlic, crushed
2 teaspoons ground allspice
¼ cup (60ml) light soy sauce
2 tablespoons mirin
1.5kg pork neck
rice wine dressing
2 tablespoons rice wine vinegar
1 tablespoon olive oil
2 teaspoons mirin
1 teaspoon dijon mustard
potato salad
700g small kipfler potatoes, halved lengthways
1 tablespoon olive oil
2 cups (160g) shredded wombok
2 medium green apples (300g), cut into matchsticks
3 green onions, sliced thinly

1 Combine the water and sugar in small saucepan; stir over heat until sugar is dissolved. Simmer about 10 minutes or until mixture is thickened slightly. Stir in chillies, garlic, spice, sauce and mirin; cool glaze.

2 Place pork in 45cm x 34cm deep disposable aluminium barbecue dish; brush with ½ cup glaze. Cook pork in covered barbecue, using indirect heat, following manufacturer's instructions, over medium heat, 25 minutes. Turn pork; cook 20 minutes. Increase heat to high; cook, uncovered, 5 minutes, turning and brushing with remaining glaze. Remove pork from barbecue; cover loosely with foil, stand 10 minutes before slicing thickly.

3 Meanwhile, make rice wine dressing and potato salad.

4 Serve pork with potato salad.

rice wine dressing Combine ingredients in screw-top jar; shake well. Season to taste.

potato salad Combine potatoes and oil in large baking dish; cook in covered barbecue, alongside pork, about 25 minutes. Remove potatoes from barbecue; transfer to large bowl. Stir in wombok, apple, onion and rice wine dressing; season to taste.

prep + cook time 1 hour 30 minutes **serves** 8

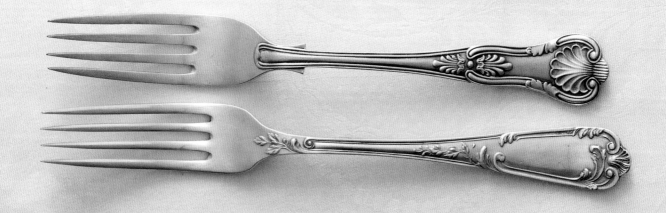

lemon and thyme roast chicken with pumpkin salad

1.5kg chicken
1 tablespoon olive oil
1 tablespoon fine salt
2 teaspoons finely cracked black pepper
2 tablespoons fresh thyme leaves
1 bulb garlic, halved crossways
1 medium lemon (140g), cut into wedges
½ bunch fresh thyme sprigs
50g butter, softened
honey mustard dressing
¼ cup (60ml) olive oil
2 tablespoons lemon juice
1 teaspoon dijon mustard
1 teaspoon honey
1 tablespoon finely chopped fresh chives
pumpkin salad
500g pumpkin, unpeeled, cut into wedges
2 tablespoons olive oil
2 bunches broccolini (350g), trimmed
1 medium red onion (170g), sliced thinly
1 tablespoon pepitas
1 tablespoon sunflower seed kernels

1 Preheat oven to 200°C/180°C fan-forced.
2 Make honey mustard dressing.
3 Wash chicken under cold water; pat dry inside and out with absorbent paper. Rub chicken with oil. Combine salt, pepper and half the thyme in small bowl; rub onto skin and inside cavity. Place garlic, lemon and thyme sprigs inside cavity.
4 Combine butter and remaining thyme in small bowl. Carefully separate skin from chicken breast with your fingers; spread butter under skin covering breast. Secure skin over cavity with fine skewers or toothpicks.
5 Place chicken on oiled wire rack in shallow roasting pan; roast, uncovered, 1 hour 20 minutes or until chicken is cooked through. Remove chicken from oven, cover loosely with foil; stand 10 minutes.
6 Meanwhile, make pumpkin salad.
7 Serve chicken with salad.
honey mustard dressing Combine ingredients in screw-top jar; shake well. Season to taste.
pumpkin salad Combine pumpkin with oil in baking dish; roast, uncovered, about 25 minutes or until browned, turning once, cool. Boil, steam or microwave broccolini until tender, drain. Combine pumpkin and broccolini with remaining ingredients and honey mustard dressing. Season to taste.

prep + cook time 2 hours **serves** 4

Sunflower seed kernels are dried husked sunflower seeds. Pepitas are dried pumpkin seeds. Both are available from health-food stores and supermarkets.

For even cooking, fold the tail of the fish under so that both ends of the salmon are roughly the same thickness. The fish can be cooked in the oven at 180°C/160°C fan-forced for about the same time.

barbecued salmon with yogurt dressing

2 medium lemons (280g) sliced thinly
1.3kg side of salmon, skin off, bones removed
2 tablespoons finely grated lemon rind
2 tablespoons finely chopped fresh flat-leaf parsley
1 cup (250ml) dry white wine
fennel salad
3 baby fennel bulbs (390g), trimmed, thinly sliced
2 tablespoons olive oil
2 teaspoons finely grated lemon rind
2 tablespoons lemon juice
400g can chickpeas, rinsed, drained
1 medium red onion (170g), sliced thinly
200g fetta cheese, cut into small cubes
80g watercress, trimmed
yogurt dressing
1 tablespoon olive oil
2 teaspoons mild harissa paste
2 tablespoons finely chopped fresh chives
¾ cup (200g) yogurt

1 Make fennel salad and yogurt dressing.
2 Place lemon slices in 45cm x 34cm deep disposable aluminium barbecue dish or shallow baking dish; top with salmon. Combine rind, parsley and wine; pour over salmon, cover with foil. Cook, in covered barbecue, using indirect heat, following manufacturer's instructions, for about 20 minutes or until cooked to your liking. Remove salmon from barbecue, cover with foil; stand 10 minutes before serving.
3 Serve salmon with salad and dressing.
fennel salad Combine fennel, oil, rind and juice; cook on heated barbecue (or grill or grill plate), turning, until fennel is tender, cool 5 minutes. Combine remaining ingredients in large bowl; stir in fennel mixture. Season to taste.
yogurt dressing Whisk ingredients in small bowl; season to taste.

prep + cook time 45 minutes **serves** 10

The secret to exceptional crackling is to ensure the pork skin is dry and well-seasoned with fine salt. Pat the pork dry with paper towel, then leave it in the fridge, uncovered, for a few hours or overnight so the skin dries out nicely before cooking.

roast pork with cranberry sauce

2kg boneless loin of pork, rind on
60g butter
1 tablespoon olive oil
1 medium red onion (170g), chopped finely
1 clove garlic, crushed
100g mild salami, chopped finely
1 tablespoon finely chopped fresh sage
¼ cup (35g) pistachios, roasted
¼ cup (35g) dried cranberries
½ cup (25g) fresh breadcrumbs
2 tablespoons fine table salt
½ cup (125ml) port
¼ cup (80g) cranberry sauce
1½ cups (375ml) chicken stock
roasted vegetables
500g pumpkin, cut into wedges
2 medium parsnips (500g), quartered
2 medium red onions (340g), quartered
500g baby carrots, trimmed
12 baby new potatoes (480g), halved
¼ cup (60ml) olive oil
2 tablespoons fresh thyme leaves

1 Preheat oven to 200°C/180°C fan-forced.
2 Using sharp knife, score pork skin by making shallow cuts at 1cm intervals. Place pork on board, fat-side down; slice through the thickest part of the pork horizontally, without cutting through the other side. Open pork out to form one large piece. Trim pork; reserve 150g trimmings for seasoning. Blend or process pork trimmings with 20g of the butter; place in large bowl.

3 Heat oil in medium frying pan; stir onion and garlic, over heat until onion is soft. Add remaining butter, salami, sage, nuts and cranberries; cook 2 minutes. Transfer mixture to medium bowl; cool. Stir in breadcrumbs and minced trimmings; season.
4 Press seasoning mixture along one long side of pork; roll pork to enclose; secure with kitchen string at 2cm intervals. Rub pork skin with salt; place on wire rack in large shallow baking dish. Roast, uncovered, about 1¼ hours or until pork is cooked through.
5 Meanwhile, cook roasted vegetables.
6 Remove pork from dish; cover pork loosely with foil, stand 15 minutes. Drain excess fat from dish, add port, sauce and stock to dish; stir over heat until sauce is reduced by half. Season to taste; cover to keep warm.
7 Serve sliced pork with sauce and vegetables.
roasted vegetables Combine vegetables in large baking dish with oil and thyme. Roast vegetables, uncovered, for last 30 minutes of pork cooking time, turning once. Season to taste.

prep + cook time 2 hours (+ standing) **serves** 8

When you order the pork loin, ask your butcher to leave a flap measuring about 20cm in length to help make rolling the seasoned loin easier.

Turkey drumsticks are available from poultry shops and most major supermarkets. Turn this recipe into a tossed salad by mixing the sliced turkey through the ingredients, rather than serving it alongside the salad.

baked turkey drumsticks with bread salad

4 turkey drumsticks (2.8kg)
2 tablespoons finely grated orange rind
¾ cup (180ml) orange juice
¼ cup (90g) honey
2 teaspoons ground turmeric
2 cloves garlic, crushed
1cm piece fresh ginger (5cm), grated
2 tablespoons sesame oil
2 tablespoons peanut oil
2 tablespoons finely chopped fresh coriander
bread salad
1 small french bread stick (150g)
⅓ cup (80ml) olive oil
2 tablespoons white balsamic vinegar
70g baby spinach leaves
1 cup loosely packed fresh basil leaves, torn
3 medium tomatoes (450g), cut into wedges
1 medium red onion (170g), sliced thickly

1   Combine drumsticks, rind, juice, honey, turmeric, garlic, ginger, oils and coriander in large bowl; cover, refrigerate 3 hours or overnight.
2   Preheat oven to 160°C/140°C fan-forced.
3   Drain drumsticks; reserve marinade. Place drumsticks on oiled wire rack in large baking dish; roast, uncovered, 1 hour 35 minutes or until cooked through, turning and basting every 20 minutes with reserved marinade. Remove drumsticks from oven, cover loosely with foil; stand 15 minutes before slicing meat from bones.
4   Meanwhile, make bread salad.
5   Serve salad with turkey.

bread salad Increase oven temperature to 200°C/180°C fan-forced. Tear bread into bite-size pieces. Toss bread and 2 tablespoons of the oil in baking dish; roast, uncovered, 10 minutes or until golden. Cool. Combine bread, remaining oil, vinegar, spinach, basil, tomato and onion in large bowl. Season to taste.

prep + cook time 2 hours (+ refrigeration) serves 6

To test if the turkey is cooked, insert a skewer sideways into the thickest part of the thigh, then remove and press flesh to release the juices. If the juice runs clear, the turkey is cooked. Alternatively, insert a meat thermometer into the thickest part of the thigh, without touching the bone; the turkey is cooked when the thermometer reaches 90°C.

roast turkey

4.5kg turkey
1 cup (250ml) water
80g butter, melted
¼ cup (35g) plain flour
3 cups (750ml) chicken stock
½ cup (125ml) dry white wine
forcemeat
40g butter
3 medium brown onions (450g), chopped finely
2 rindless bacon rashers (130g), chopped coarsely
1 cup (70g) stale breadcrumbs
½ cup coarsely chopped fresh flat-leaf parsley
250g pork mince
250g chicken mince

1 Preheat oven to 180°C/160°C fan-forced.

2 Make forcemeat.

3 Discard neck from turkey. Rinse turkey under cold water; pat dry inside and out with absorbent paper. Fill neck cavity loosely with forcemeat; secure skin over opening with small skewers. Fill large cavity loosely with forcemeat; tie legs together with kitchen string.

4 Place turkey on oiled wire rack in large shallow baking dish; pour the water into dish. Brush turkey all over with half the butter; cover turkey tightly with two layers of greased foil. Roast 2 hours.

5 Uncover turkey; brush with remaining butter. Roast, turkey, uncovered, about 1 hour or until cooked through. Remove turkey from dish, cover loosely with foil; stand 20 minutes.

6 Pour juice from dish into large jug; skim 1 tablespoon of fat from juice, return fat to same dish. Skim and discard fat from remaining juice; reserve juice. Add flour to dish; cook, stirring, until mixture bubbles and is well-browned. Gradually stir in stock, wine and reserved juice; cook, stirring, until gravy boils and thickens. Strain gravy into jug; serve with turkey.

forcemeat Melt butter in medium frying pan; cook onion and bacon, stirring, over low heat, until onion is soft, cool. Combine onion mixture and remaining ingredients in large bowl; season to taste.

prep + cook time 3 hours 45 minutes (+ standing)
serves 8

Ask the butcher to butterfly the turkey for you. The turkey can be cooked in the oven, if you prefer. Preheat oven to 180°C/160°C fan-forced and cook, uncovered, on wire rack, for about 1¾ hours.

barbecued butterflied turkey with vegetable salad

3kg turkey
1 chorizo sausage (170g), chopped finely
½ cup (75g) finely chopped drained sun-dried
    tomatoes in oil
½ cup coarsely chopped fresh flat-leaf parsley
½ cup (50g) hazelnut meal
vegetable salad
3 small zucchini (270g), sliced thinly
3 baby eggplants (180g), sliced thinly
16 flat mushrooms (1.3kg), trimmed
1 tablespoon finely chopped fresh rosemary
1 tablespoon finely chopped fresh basil
⅓ cup (80ml) olive oil
2 tablespoons balsamic vinegar
80g mixed salad leaves

1 Place turkey, breast-side down, on board. Using kitchen scissors, cut down either side of backbone, discard backbone. Turn turkey skin-side up; press down on breastbone with heel of hand to flatten. Season.
2 Combine chorizo, tomatoes, parsley and meal in medium bowl; season to taste. Using fingers, carefully pull skin away from meat on breasts and thighs of turkey. Push chorizo mixture evenly under the skin.
3 Place turkey in deep disposable aluminium barbecue dish or baking dish; cook turkey in covered barbecue, using indirect heat, following manufacturer's instructions, over low heat for about 1¾ hours. Remove from barbecue; cover loosely with foil, stand 15 minutes.
4 Make vegetable salad.
5 Serve turkey with salad.
vegetable salad Combine zucchini, eggplant, mushrooms, rosemary, basil and half the oil in large bowl. Cook vegetables, in batches, on heated barbecue (or grill plate) until tender. Combine remaining oil and vinegar in screw-top jar; shake well. Combine vegetables, salad leaves and dressing in large bowl; toss gently, season to taste.

prep + cook time 2 hours 30 minutes (+ standing)
serves 8

You need to buy 600g fresh peas in the pod to get the amount of shelled peas needed for this recipe, or use frozen peas, if preferred.
If you buy thin fresh young asparagus, you don't have to cook it. It will add an earthy nutty texture to the salad.
Use the rind from the ham to cover the cut surface; this will keep the ham moist during storage.

glazed ham with asparagus salad

½ cup (180g) honey
½ cup (125ml) maple syrup
½ cup (110g) firmly packed brown sugar
2¼ cups (560ml) water
7kg cooked leg of ham
cider mustard dressing
⅓ cup (80ml) cider vinegar
2 teaspoons dijon mustard
2 cloves garlic, crushed
2 tablespoons finely chopped fresh chives
½ cup (125ml) olive oil
asparagus salad
680g asparagus spears, trimmed
2 tablespoons olive oil
2 cups (320g) shelled fresh peas
4 witlof (500g), leaves separated
200g mixed salad leaves

1 Preheat oven to 180°C/160°C fan-forced.
2 Combine honey, syrup, sugar and ¼ cup of the water in small saucepan; stir over heat until sugar dissolves. Bring to the boil; remove from heat, cool 10 minutes.
3 Cut through rind of ham 10cm from the shank end of the leg. To remove rind, run thumb around edge of rind just under skin. Start pulling rind from widest edge of ham, continue to pull rind carefully away from the fat up to the shank end. Remove rind completely. Score across the fat at about 3cm intervals, cutting lightly through the surface of the fat (not the meat) in a diamond pattern.
4 Pour the remaining water into a large baking dish; place ham on oiled wire rack over dish. Brush ham all over with honey glaze. Roast, uncovered, 1 hour or until browned, brushing frequently with glaze during cooking.
5 Make cider mustard dressing and asparagus salad.
6 Serve sliced ham with salad.
cider mustard dressing Combine ingredients in screw-top jar; shake well. Season to taste.
asparagus salad Combine asparagus with oil in medium bowl; cook asparagus on heated barbecue (or grill or grill plate) until tender. Boil, steam or microwave peas until tender. Combine asparagus with peas and remaining ingredients in large bowl; stir in cider mustard dressing

prep + cook time 1 hour 20 minutes serves 16

rare roast beef with anchovy butter

½ cup (125ml) barbecue sauce
2 cloves garlic, crushed
1 tablespoon finely chopped fresh rosemary
⅓ cup (80ml) olive oil
2kg boneless beef sirloin
300g butter beans, trimmed
300g green beans, trimmed
800g button mushrooms
2 tablespoons finely chopped fresh chives
anchovy butter
200g butter, softened
4 shallots (100g), chopped finely
1 tablespoon dijon mustard
1 tablespoon finely chopped fresh tarragon
5 drained anchovy fillets, chopped finely
1 teaspoon ground sumac

1 Preheat oven to 220°C/200°C fan-forced.
2 Make anchovy butter.
3 Combine sauce, garlic, rosemary and 2 tablespoons of the oil in small bowl; rub all over beef. Place beef on oiled wire rack over baking dish; pour in enough water to half fill the dish. Roast beef 45 minutes or until cooked to your liking. Remove beef from heat, cover loosely with foil; stand 10 minutes before slicing thickly.
4 Boil, steam or microwave beans until tender; drain. Heat remaining oil in large frying pan, add mushrooms; stir over medium heat until tender. Combine mushrooms and beans in large bowl; stir in chives, season to taste.
5 Serve beef topped with slices of anchovy butter; accompany with mushroom and bean mixture.
anchovy butter Beat butter in medium bowl with electric mixer until soft; beat in remaining ingredients, season to taste. Form into log, roll in plastic wrap; refrigerate or freeze until firm.

prep + cook time 1 hour 25 minutes (+ refrigeration)
serves 8

Sumac is available from supermarkets and spice shops.

Moroccan spice mix consists of coriander seed, turmeric, paprika, cumin, ginger, cloves, allspice, pepper and chilli. It is available from supermarkets as well as Middle-Eastern food stores and spice shops.

char-grilled lamb with pistachio and fig couscous

6 x 200g lamb backstraps, trimmed
2 tablespoons olive oil
2 cloves garlic, crushed
2 tablespoons moroccan spice mix
pistachio and fig couscous
2 cups (500ml) chicken stock
1 teaspoon sea salt
2 tablespoons olive oil
2 cups (400g) couscous
1 tablespoon finely grated lemon rind
2 tablespoons lemon juice
1 medium red onion (170g), chopped finely
½ cup (70g) pistachios
½ cup (100g) coarsely chopped dried figs
2 tablespoons coarsely chopped fresh flat-leaf parsley
80g baby spinach leaves

1   Combine lamb, oil, garlic and spice in large bowl. Cover; refrigerate 3 hours or overnight.
2   Cook lamb on heated oiled barbecue (or grill or grill plate) until cooked to your liking. Cover lamb loosely with foil; stand 5 minutes then slice thickly.
3   Meanwhile make pistachio and fig couscous.
4   Top couscous with lamb, serve with lemon wedges.
pistachio and fig couscous Combine stock, salt and oil in small saucepan; bring to the boil. Combine couscous, rind, juice and onion in large bowl; add hot stock. Cover; stand about 10 minutes or until liquid is absorbed, fluffing with fork occasionally. Mix in nuts, figs, parsley and spinach; season to taste.

prep + cook time 40 minutes (+ refrigeration) **serves** 6

You can tell if fish is cooked by checking to see if the flesh is flaking away from the skin. A 180g to 200g fish portion should take about 6 minutes to cook plus 5 minutes resting when cooked in this style. We used blue-eye fillets in this recipe.

crisp-skinned fish with mustard butter

¼ cup (60ml) olive oil
6 x 200g white fish fillets, skin on
1 small red onion (100g), chopped finely
2 chorizo sausages (340g), chopped coarsely
250g cherry tomatoes, halved
440g can cannellini beans, rinsed, drained
200g baby spinach leaves
mustard butter
125g butter, softened
2 teaspoons dijon mustard
2 teaspoons wholegrain mustard
½ teaspoon ground paprika
1 tablespoon finely grated lemon rind
1 tablespoon finely chopped fresh flat-leaf parsley

1   Preheat oven to 200°C/180°C fan-forced.
2   Make mustard butter.
3   Heat 2 tablespoons of the oil in large frying pan; cook fish, skin-side down, in batches, until skin is crisp. Transfer fish, skin-side up, to foil-lined oven tray; roast, in oven, 6 minutes or until fish is cooked to your liking. Remove from oven, cover loosely with foil; stand 5 minutes.
4   Meanwhile, heat remaining oil in same cleaned large pan; cook onion over medium heat, stirring, until soft. Add chorizo; cook, stirring, 1 minute. Stir in tomato and beans. Reduce heat; cook about 2 minutes or until beans are heated through. Stir in spinach; season to taste.
5   Serve bean mixture topped with fish and a slice of mustard butter.

mustard butter Beat butter in small bowl with electric mixer until soft. Beat in remaining ingredients; season to taste. Form mixture into log, roll in plastic wrap; refrigerate or freeze until firm.

prep + cook time 40 minutes (+ refrigeration) **serves** 6

Buy individual tuna steaks instead of the fillet, if you prefer. Cook steaks for about 5 minutes; the time will depend on their thickness.

seared tuna with verjuice dressing

2 tablespoons hot english mustard
¼ cup (60ml) light soy sauce
1 tablespoon peanut oil
800g piece tuna fillet
8 baby new potatoes (320g), halved
250g green beans, trimmed
1 cup (150g) seeded black olives
250g cherry tomatoes, halved
1 small red onion (100g), cut into wedges
6 medium-boiled eggs, halved
verjuice dressing
2 tablespoons verjuice
1 tablespoon dijon mustard
¼ cup (60ml) walnut oil
1 tablespoon finely chopped fresh chervil

1 Make verjuice dressing.
2 Combine mustard, sauce, oil and tuna in large bowl. Cover, refrigerate 3 hours or overnight.
3 Boil, steam or microwave potato and beans, separately, until tender; drain. Combine potato, beans, olives, tomato, onion and dressing in large bowl; toss gently. Top with eggs; season to taste.
4 Remove tuna from marinade; discard marinade. Cook tuna on preheated barbecue (or grill or grill plate) about 10 minutes, turning, until marked well on all sides and cooked to your liking. Remove from heat, cover loosely with foil; stand 10 minutes.
5 Cut tuna into slices; serve with salad.
verjuice dressing Combine ingredients in screw-top jar; shake well. Season to taste.

prep + cook time 40 minutes (+ refrigeration) **serves** 6

Verjuice is an unfermented grape juice with a fresh lemony-vinegar flavour. It's available in supermarkets, usually in the vinegar section.

rib eye steaks with sweet potato and coleslaw

½ cup (110g) firmly packed brown sugar
¾ cup (180ml) stout
2 tablespoons worcestershire sauce
6 x 350g beef rib-eye steaks
1 large kumara (500g), sliced thinly
2 tablespoons olive oil
80g baby rocket leaves
coleslaw
2 cups (160g) red cabbage, shredded finely
2 cups (160g) green cabbage, shredded finely
1 medium carrot (120g), sliced thinly
1 tablespoon finely grated lemon rind
1 tablespoon lemon juice
½ teaspoon cayenne pepper
½ cup (150g) mayonnaise
2 tablespoons warm water

1 Combine sugar, stout and sauce in large bowl, add beef; turn to coat beef in marinade. Cover bowl; refrigerate 3 hours or overnight.
2 Make coleslaw.
3 Remove beef from marinade; cook on heated barbecue (or grill or grill plate) until cooked to your liking. Remove beef from heat, cover loosely with foil; stand 10 minutes.
4 Meanwhile, toss kumara with oil in large bowl; cook on heated barbecue until tender, season to taste.
5 Serve beef with kumara, coleslaw and rocket.
coleslaw Combine ingredients in large bowl; season to taste.

prep + cook time 40 minutes (+ refrigeration)
serves 6

You can use either savoy cabbage or wombok (also known as chinese cabbage) in the coleslaw. Stout is a strong tasting dark-coloured beer that goes well with beef.

Ask the fishmonger to clean the baby octopus for you, or buy prepared baby octopus, instead. Octopus should be cooked quickly over a high heat until they turn opaque – over-cooking will toughen them.

barbecued baby octopus with greek-style salad

1kg baby octopus, cleaned
⅓ cup (80ml) balsamic vinegar
½ cup (125ml) olive oil
2 cloves garlic, crushed
2 fresh small red thai chillies, sliced thinly
3 teaspoons coarsely chopped fresh rosemary
1 tablespoon finely grated lemon rind
1 tablespoon lemon juice
700g kipfler potatoes, halved lengthways
basil dressing
1 cup (200g) crumbled fetta cheese
2 tablespoons olive oil
¼ cup (60ml) cream
2 teaspoons finely grated lemon rind
2 teaspoons lemon juice
1 cup loosely packed fresh basil leaves
greek-style salad
2 lebanese cucumbers (260g), seeded,
    chopped coarsely
1 medium red onion (170g), chopped coarsely
4 large tomatoes (880g), chopped coarsely
50g baby rocket leaves

1 Combine octopus, vinegar, ⅓ cup of the oil, garlic, chilli, rosemary, rind and juice in large bowl. Cover; refrigerate 2 hours.
2 Make basil dressing; make greek-style salad.
3 Boil, steam or microwave potato until tender; drain. Toss potato in remaining oil. Cook on heated barbecue until browned lightly and tender. Transfer potato to large bowl; toss with half the dressing.
4 Remove octopus from marinade, discard marinade. Cook octopus on heated oiled barbecue (or grill or grill plate) until changed in colour.
5 Serve octopus with potato and salad; drizzle with remaining dressing.
basil dressing Process cheese, oil, cream, rind and juice until smooth. Add basil; process until combined.
greek-style salad Combine ingredients in large bowl; season to taste.

prep + cook time 30 minutes (+ refrigeration)
serves 6

Puddings

The big day wouldn't be complete without a pudding of some sort. If there's a large crowd, especially where you have a range of different age groups, it's a good idea to serve both a hot pudding – either traditional, or one of the quirky modern pudding recipes in this chapter – with a lovely sauce, as well as a cold dessert. Make life easier for yourself by choosing a recipe that can be made well ahead of the big day.

orange, date and treacle pudding

1 cup (150g) finely chopped dried dates
⅓ cup (80ml) orange juice, warmed
60g butter
¼ cup (90g) treacle
½ teaspoon bicarbonate of soda
1 cup (150g) self-raising flour
1 teaspoon mixed spice
⅓ cup (80ml) milk
1 egg

orange syrup
¼ cup (55g) caster sugar
2 tablespoons treacle
1 teaspoon finely grated orange rind
¼ cup (60ml) orange juice
25g butter

1 Grease 2-litre (8-cup) pudding steamer.
2 Combine dates and juice in small bowl; cover, stand 20 minutes.
3 Melt butter with treacle in small saucepan. Remove from heat, stir in soda; transfer mixture to medium bowl. Stir in sifted flour and spice, then combined milk and egg, in two batches. Stir in date mixture.
4 Spread mixture into steamer. Cover with pleated baking paper and foil; secure with lid.
5 Place pudding steamer in large saucepan with enough boiling water to come halfway up side of steamer; cover pan with tight-fitting lid. Boil 1 hour, replenishing with boiling water as necessary to maintain water level. Remove pudding; stand 5 minutes before turning onto a plate.
6 Meanwhile, make orange syrup. Serve pudding with orange syrup.
orange syrup Combine ingredients in small saucepan; stir over medium heat until smooth. Bring to the boil, reduce heat; simmer, uncovered, 2 minutes.

---

prep + cook time 1 hour 15 minutes (+ standing)
serves 8

The pudding is at its best made on the day and served hot.

frozen tiramisu terrine

4 egg yolks

2 eggs

½ cup (110g) caster sugar

300ml cream

250g mascarpone cheese

2 tablespoons marsala

450g packet rectangular unfilled sponge slabs

1 tablespoon instant coffee granules

2 tablespoons boiling water

100g dark eating chocolate, grated coarsely

ganache

100g dark eating chocolate, chopped finely

⅓ cup (80ml) cream

1   Grease 21cm x 14cm loaf pan; line with baking paper, extending 5cm over two long sides.

2   Combine egg yolks, eggs and sugar in medium heatproof bowl set over medium saucepan of simmering water. Using electric mixer, beat mixture 5 minutes or until thick and creamy. Remove from heat; cool.

3   Meanwhile, beat cream, mascarpone and marsala in small bowl with electric mixer until soft peaks form; transfer to large bowl. Fold egg mixture into mascarpone mixture; refrigerate 1 hour.

4   Meanwhile, make ganache.

5   Trim and discard crusts from all sides of both sponges. Split each sponge in half; trim to fit pan as needed during the layering process. Brush sponge slices with combined coffee and the boiling water. Spread half the mascarpone mixture into loaf pan; drizzle with half of the cooled ganache, top with half the sponge. Repeat layers with remaining mascarpone mixture, ganache and sponge. Cover; freeze overnight. Remove terrine from pan; turn onto plate, discard paper. Serve slices of terrine topped with chocolate.

ganache Stir chocolate and cream in small saucepan over low heat until smooth; cool.

----

prep + cook time 45 minutes
(+ refrigeration and freezing) **serves** 10

This terrine can be made and frozen three days ahead.

black forest trifle

2 x 425g cans seeded black cherries in syrup
⅓ cup (80ml) cherry brandy
350g frozen chocolate cake
2 teaspoons gelatine
2 tablespoons water
chocolate custard
⅓ cup (75g) caster sugar
2 tablespoons cornflour
1 cup (250ml) milk
300ml cream
125g dark eating chocolate, chopped finely
mascarpone cream
250g mascarpone cheese
300ml cream
2 tablespoons icing sugar

1   Make chocolate custard.
2   Drain cherries; reserve syrup (you need 1¼ cups). Combine brandy and drained cherries in small bowl.
3   Discard icing from cake if necessary; chop cake into 2cm pieces.
4   Divide cake into eight 1½-cup (375ml) serving glasses. Spoon cherry mixture over cake; top with warm custard; refrigerate 30 minutes.

5   Make mascarpone cream. Spread mascarpone cream over custard; refrigerate 15 minutes.
6   Sprinkle gelatine over the water in small heatproof jug; stand jug in small saucepan of simmering water. Stir until gelatine dissolves; cool 5 minutes. Stir gelatine into reserved cherry syrup. Refrigerate 20 minutes. Top trifles with cherry jelly; refrigerate 3 hours or until jelly sets. Top with extra fresh cherries, if you like.
chocolate custard Blend sugar and cornflour in medium saucepan; gradually whisk in milk and cream. Stir over medium heat until custard boils and thickens. Remove from heat; stir in chocolate until smooth.
mascarpone cream Beat ingredients in small bowl with electric mixer until soft peaks form.

----

prep + cook time 40 minutes (+ refrigeration)
serves 8

Trifles can be made a day ahead; keep refrigerated overnight.

The whole orange in the middle of the pudding might make the pudding a little soggy – it's caused by the moisture in the orange – don't worry, it tastes delicious. Use a serrated knife to cut the pudding. We used Cointreau in this recipe, but you can use your favourite citrus-flavoured liqueur.

jaffa steamed pudding

1 small orange (180g)
2½ cups (625ml) water
1½ cups (330g) caster sugar
100g butter, chopped coarsely
100g dark eating chocolate, chopped coarsely
1¼ cups (185g) self-raising flour
¼ cup (25g) cocoa powder
⅔ cup (80g) almond meal
2 eggs, beaten lightly
1 teaspoon finely grated orange rind
¼ cup (60ml) orange juice
chocolate sauce
125g dark eating chocolate, chopped coarsely
⅔ cup (160ml) cream
1 tablespoon citrus-flavoured liqueur

1 Combine orange and the water in medium saucepan, bring to the boil; boil 10 minutes. Stir in ¾ cup of the sugar. Return to the boil; reduce heat, simmer 5 minutes. Remove from the heat; stand orange in poaching liquid for 10 minutes. Remove orange; discard liquid. Prick orange all over with a skewer.

2 Combine butter and chocolate in small saucepan; stir over low heat until smooth, cool 5 minutes. Stir in remaining sugar, then sifted flour and cocoa, meal, eggs, rind and juice. Spread half the mixture into well greased 1.5-litre (6-cup) pudding steamer. Using the back of a spoon, make a hollow in the centre of the mixture. Sit orange in hollow; spread remaining mixture over orange. Cover steamer with pleated baking paper and foil; secure with lid.

3 Place steamer in large saucepan with enough boiling water to come halfway up side of steamer; cover pan with tight-fitting lid. Boil 2½ hours, replenishing with boiling water as necessary to maintain water level. Remove pudding; stand 5 minutes before turning onto plate.

4 Meanwhile, make chocolate sauce.

5 Serve pudding drizzled with warm sauce, and cream, if you like.

chocolate sauce Combine chocolate and cream in small saucepan; stir over low heat until smooth. Stir in liqueur.

prep + cook time 2 hours 15 minutes serves 8

This recipe will make two smaller puddings; use two 40cm-squares of calico to make the smaller puddings. Boil puddings in separate boilers for 2 hours. If you only have one boiler, the pudding mixture will stand at room temperature while you cook the first one.

golden boiled pudding

1 cup (180g) finely chopped dried pears
1 cup (130g) finely chopped dried cranberries
1 cup (75g) finely chopped dried apples
½ cup (80g) finely chopped dried apricots
1 large apple (200g), peeled, grated
⅓ cup (80ml) orange-flavoured liqueur
2 teaspoons finely grated orange rind
2 tablespoons orange juice
250g butter, softened
1½ cups (330g) caster sugar
4 eggs
1 cup (150g) plain flour
½ teaspoon bicarbonate of soda
1 teaspoon ground cinnamon
3 cups (210g) stale breadcrumbs
1 cup (120g) almond meal
⅔ cup (100g) plain flour, extra

1   Combine fruit, liqueur, rind and juice in large bowl. Cover, stand at room temperature overnight.
2   Beat butter and sugar in small bowl with electric mixer until combined; beat in eggs one at a time. Mix butter mixture into fruit mixture. Mix in sifted flour, soda and cinnamon, then breadcrumbs and meal.
3   Fill boiler three-quarters full of hot water, cover with tight lid; bring to the boil. Have ready 1-metre length of kitchen string and extra plain flour. Wearing thick rubber gloves, dip pudding cloth into boiling water. Boil 1 minute then remove; squeeze excess water from cloth. Quickly spread hot cloth on bench. Rub flour into centre of cloth to cover an area about 40cm in diameter, leaving flour a little thicker in centre of cloth where "skin" on pudding needs to be thickest.
4   Place pudding mixture in centre of cloth. Gather cloth evenly around mixture, avoiding any deep pleats; pat into round shape. Tie cloth tightly with string as close to mixture as possible. Pull ends of cloth tightly to ensure pudding is as round and as firm as possible; tie loops in string.
5   Lower pudding into the boiling water; tie ends of string to handles of boiler to suspend pudding. Cover with tight lid; boil 3 hours, replenishing with boiling water as necessary to maintain water level.
6   Untie pudding from handles; place wooden spoon through string loops. Do not put pudding on bench; suspend from spoon by placing over rungs of upturned stool or wedging handle in a drawer. Twist ends of cloth around string to avoid them touching pudding; hang pudding for 10 minutes.
7   Place pudding on board; cut string, carefully peel back cloth. Turn pudding onto a plate then carefully peel cloth away completely; cool. Stand at least 20 minutes or until skin darkens and pudding becomes firm. Serve dusted with icing sugar, if you like.

prep + cook time 3 hours 40 minutes (+ standing)
serves 16

You need a 60cm-square of unbleached calico for the pudding cloth. If calico has not been used before, soak it in cold water overnight; the next day, boil it for 20 minutes then rinse in cold water.
We used Grand Marnier, but you can use your favourite orange-flavoured liqueur.

baklava cheesecake

⅓ cup (35g) walnuts
⅔ cup (90g) pistachios
2 teaspoons mixed spice
250g butternut snap cookies
½ cup (70g) slivered almonds
125g unsalted butter, melted
cheesecake filling
3 teaspoons gelatine
¼ cup (60ml) water
500g packaged cream cheese, softened
½ cup (110g) caster sugar
¼ cup (90g) honey
1½ cups (375ml) thickened cream

1   Preheat oven to 220°C/200°C fan-forced. Grease 26cm springform tin.
2   Roast walnuts and pistachios on oven tray about 5 minutes. Sprinkle nuts with spice; roast 1 minute, cool. Process nuts with cookies until chopped finely; transfer to medium bowl, stir in almonds.
3   Set aside one-third of the nut mixture. Stir butter into remaining nut mixture. Press mixture evenly over base of tin; refrigerate 30 minutes.
4   Meanwhile, make cheesecake filling.
5   Pour cheesecake filling into tin; sprinkle top with reserved nut mixture. Cover; refrigerate overnight.
cheesecake filling Sprinkle gelatine over the water in small heatproof jug; stand jug in small saucepan of simmering water. Stir until gelatine dissolves, cool 5 minutes. Beat cream cheese, sugar and honey in medium bowl with electric mixer until smooth; beat in cream, then stir in gelatine mixture.

prep + cook time 35 minutes (+ refrigeration) **serves** 16

Cheesecake can be made a day ahead; keep, covered, in the fridge.

glacé fruit puddings with ginger syrup

100g butter, softened
1 teaspoon finely grated lemon rind
¾ cup (165g) caster sugar
2 eggs
½ cup (75g) plain flour
½ cup (75g) self-raising flour
½ cup (60g) almond meal
⅓ cup (80ml) milk
4 slices (110g) glacé pineapple, chopped finely
⅓ cup (85g) finely chopped glacé apricots
⅓ cup (85g) finely chopped glacé figs
ginger syrup
½ cup (125ml) water
½ cup (110g) caster sugar
2cm piece fresh ginger (10g), grated

1 Preheat oven to 180°C/160°C fan-forced. Grease six ¾-cup (180ml) pudding moulds or ovenproof tea cups; place on oven tray.
2 Beat butter, rind and sugar in small bowl with electric mixer until light and fluffy. Beat in eggs, one at a time.
3 Transfer mixture to medium bowl; stir in sifted flours, meal, milk and fruit. Spread mixture into pudding moulds; bake about 35 minutes.
4 Meanwhile, make ginger syrup.
5 Remove puddings from oven; pour hot syrup over hot puddings in moulds. Stand 5 minutes before turning onto serving plates (or serve in tea cups). Serve warm.
ginger syrup Combine ingredients in small saucepan; stir over low heat, without boiling, until sugar dissolves. Bring to the boil, reduce heat, simmer, uncovered, without stirring, about 3 minutes or until syrup thickens slightly.

prep + cook time 50 minutes serves 6

Puddings are best made just before serving. The mixture may curdle when the second egg is added, however, it will become smooth again once the flour is stirred in.

We used Cointreau in this recipe, but you can use any citrus-flavoured liqueur. The seeded vanilla pod can be pushed into a jar of caster sugar and used for baking. The pod will impart a vanilla flavour into the sugar. Instead of using mixed fresh berries, use your favourite berry in the flan.

berry custard flan

1 cup (250ml) milk
¾ cup (180ml) cream
1 vanilla bean
3 egg yolks
⅓ cup (75g) caster sugar
¼ cup (35g) cornflour
25g unsalted butter
500g mixed fresh berries
2 tablespoons raspberry jam, warmed, strained
1 tablespoon citrus-flavoured liqueur
pastry
1¼ cups (185g) plain flour
¼ cup (55g) caster sugar
125g cold unsalted butter, chopped coarsely
1 egg yolk

1   Make pastry.
2   Roll pastry between sheets of baking paper large enough to line 22cm-round, 2.5cm-deep, loose-based flan tin. Ease pastry into tin; press into side, trim edge. Prick base all over with fork. Cover, refrigerate 30 minutes.
3   Preheat oven to 200°C/180°C fan-forced.
4   Place tin on oven tray, line with baking paper; fill with dried beans or rice. Bake 12 minutes; remove paper and beans carefully from tin. Bake 5 minutes or until pastry is browned lightly; cool 15 minutes.
5   Meanwhile, combine milk and cream in small saucepan. Split vanilla bean in half, scrape seeds into pan; bring to the boil. Beat egg yolks, sugar and cornflour in small bowl with electric mixer until thick and creamy. Gradually beat hot milk mixture into egg mixture. Return mixture to pan; cook, stirring, until mixture boils and thickens. Stir in butter. Pour warm custard into pastry case; cover, refrigerate 3 hours.
6   Serve flan topped with berries; drizzle with combined jam and liqueur.
pastry   Process flour, sugar and butter until crumbly. Add egg yolk; process until combined. Knead on floured surface until smooth. Wrap pastry in plastic, refrigerate 30 minutes.

prep + cook time 45 minutes
(+ refrigeration and cooling) **serves** 12

Ice-cream can be made three days ahead. Praline can be pressed onto the ice-cream up to a day in advance. Cover tightly with plastic wrap and freeze until required.

burnt brown sugar ice-cream with pistachio praline

¾ cup (165g) firmly packed brown sugar
¼ cup (60ml) orange juice
1¾ cups (430ml) milk
600ml cream
8 egg yolks
pistachio praline
¾ cup (165g) caster sugar
⅓ cup (80ml) water
⅓ cup (45g) pistachios, roasted

1   Combine sugar and juice in medium saucepan; stir over heat, without boiling, until sugar dissolves. Bring to the boil; reduce heat, simmer, uncovered, without stirring, about 7 minutes or until mixture is dark brown in colour. Remove from heat, gradually stir in combined milk and cream; stir over heat until toffee dissolves and mixture is smooth.

2   Using electric mixer, beat egg yolks in medium bowl until thick and creamy; gradually beat in hot milk mixture. Pour mixture into large saucepan; stir over low heat, without boiling, until mixture thickens slightly and coats the back of a wooden spoon.

3   Immediately strain custard mixture into medium heatproof bowl. Cover surface of custard with plastic wrap; refrigerate 1 hour or until cold.

4   To make ice-cream, pour custard into a shallow container, such as an aluminium slab cake pan, cover with foil; freeze until almost firm. Place custard mixture in large bowl, chop coarsely then beat with electric mixer until smooth. Pour into deep container, cover; freeze until firm. Repeat process twice more; pour into 2-litre (8-cup) pudding bowl after last beating. (Or pour custard into ice-cream maker, churn according to manufacturer's instructions). Freeze until firm.

5   Meanwhile, make pistachio praline.

6   Dip pudding bowl into hot water for 10 seconds; turn ice-cream onto plate. Press pistachio praline all over ice-cream to coat; freeze 1 hour before serving.

pistachio praline Combine sugar and the water in small saucepan; stir over heat, without boiling, until sugar dissolves. Bring to the boil; boil 5 minutes or until golden caramel in colour. Place nuts on oiled oven tray; pour toffee over nuts, stand until set. Break praline into small pieces; process until chopped finely.

prep + cook time 50 minutes
(+ refrigeration and freezing) **serves** 8

This recipe makes six generous single servings. You need six 30cm squares of unbleached calico for each pudding cloth. If the calico has not been used before, soak it in cold water overnight; the next day, boil it for 20 minutes then rinse in cold water. Puddings can be cooked in two boilers or in batches; the mixture will keep at room temperature for several hours.

mini Christmas puddings

1 cup (150g) raisins, chopped coarsely
1 cup (160g) sultanas
1 cup (150g) finely chopped seeded dried dates
½ cup (95g) finely chopped seeded prunes
½ cup (85g) mixed peel
½ cup (125g) finely chopped glacé apricots
1 teaspoon finely grated lemon rind
2 tablespoons lemon juice
2 tablespoons apricot jam
2 tablespoons brandy
250g butter, softened
2 cups (440g) firmly packed brown sugar
5 eggs
1¼ cups (185g) plain flour
½ teaspoon ground nutmeg
½ teaspoon mixed spice
4 cups (280g) stale breadcrumbs
1 cup (150g) plain flour, extra
6 x 30cm squares unbleached calico

1   Combine fruit, rind, juice, jam and brandy in large bowl. Cover with plastic wrap; stand in cool, dark place for one week, stirring every day.
2   Beat butter and sugar in small bowl with electric mixer until combined; beat in eggs one at a time. Stir butter mixture into fruit mixture. Stir in sifted dry ingredients and breadcrumbs.
3   Fill boiler three-quarters full of hot water, cover with tight lid; bring to the boil. Have ready 1-metre length of kitchen string and extra flour. Wearing thick rubber gloves, dip pudding cloths, one at a time, into boiling water; boil 1 minute then remove, squeeze excess water from cloth. Spread hot cloths on bench; rub 2 tablespoons of the extra flour into centre of each cloth to cover an area about 18cm in diameter, leaving flour a little thicker in centre of cloth where "skin" on the pudding needs to be thickest.
4   Divide pudding mixture equally among cloths; placing in centre of each cloth. Gather cloths around mixture, avoiding any deep pleats; pat into round shapes. Tie cloths tightly with string as close to mixture as possible. Tie loops in string. Lower three puddings into the boiling water. Cover, boil 2 hours, replenishing with boiling water as necessary to maintain water level.
5   Lift puddings from water using wooden spoons through string loops. Do not put puddings on bench; suspend from spoon by placing over rungs of upturned stool or wedging the spoon in a drawer. Twist ends of cloth around string to avoid them touching puddings; hang 10 minutes. Repeat with remaining puddings.
6   Place puddings on board; cut string, carefully peel back cloth. Turn puddings onto plates then carefully peel cloth away completely; cool. Stand at least 20 minutes or until skin darkens and pudding becomes firm.

prep + cook time 2 hours 50 minutes (+ standing)
makes 6

Top puddings with a slice of glacé orange, if you like. It is available from gourmet and health-food stores.

brandy butter

Beat 125g soft unsalted butter in small bowl with electric mixer until as white as possible. Beat in ¼ cup sifted icing sugar and 2 tablespoons brandy until light and fluffy.

----

prep time 10 minutes
makes 1 cup **serves** 8

brandy custard

Combine 300ml thickened cream, 1 tablespoon sifted icing sugar and seeds from 1 vanilla bean in small bowl; beat with electric mixer until soft peaks form. Stir 500g tub thick custard and 2 tablespoons brandy in small saucepan over low heat until warm. Transfer to large bowl; gently fold cream mixture into warm custard.

----

prep + cook time 10 minutes
makes 3½ cups **serves** 8

hard sauce

Beat 250g softened unsalted butter and 2 cups sifted icing sugar in small bowl with electric mixer until as white as possible. Beat in ¼ cup cream and 2 tablespoons brandy.

----

prep time 10 minutes
makes 2 cups **serves** 12

star anise and orange custard

Bring 2 cups milk, 300ml cream, 3 star anise and 10cm strip orange rind to the boil in medium saucepan. Remove from heat; stand 10 minutes. Discard star anise and rind. Beat 6 egg yolks and ½ cup caster sugar in medium bowl with electric mixer until thick and creamy; gradually beat in warm milk mixture. Return custard to pan; stir over low heat, without boiling, until mixture is thick enough to coat the back of a spoon. Stir in 2 tablespoons orange-flavoured liqueur. Serve warm or cold.

prep + cook time 20 minutes
makes 4 cups **serves** 12

We used Grand Marnier liqueur in this recipe; you can use any orange-flavoured liqueur you like.

eggnog custard

Bring 1¼ cups milk and 2 teaspoons instant coffee granules to the boil in small saucepan. Beat 4 egg yolks and ⅓ cup caster sugar in small bowl with electric mixer until thick and creamy; gradually beat in hot milk mixture. Return custard mixture to pan; stir, over low heat, without boiling, until mixture is thick enough to coat the back of a spoon. Stir in 2 tablespoons bourbon.

prep + cook time 15 minutes
makes 1½ cups **serves** 6

hazelnut liqueur ice-cream sauce

Melt 1½ cups softened full-cream vanilla ice-cream in medium saucepan over low heat. Blend 3 teaspoons cornflour with 1 tablespoon cold water; whisk into ice-cream. Stir over heat until mixture boils and thickens. Pour mixture into large bowl; whisk in ¼ cup hazelnut-flavoured liqueur; cool. Beat 1¾ cups thickened cream in small bowl with electric mixer until soft peaks form; whisk half the cream into ice-cream mixture then fold in remaining cream.

prep + cook time 15 minutes
makes 1 litre (4 cups) **serves** 12

We used Frangelico liqueur in this recipe; or try either a chocolate- or orange-flavoured liqueur, if you like.

81

Baking

Christmas just wouldn't be Christmas without some serious baking being done. Cakes and other baked goodies make wonderful gifts; they're always appreciated as everyone knows that baking takes time and effort. It's a good idea to include a copy of the recipe you've used with the gift, in case you've used an ingredient that might not suit everyone's tastes, dietary requirements or allergies.

pomegranate cookies

250g butter, softened
1 cup (160g) icing sugar
2 cups (300g) plain flour
½ cup (75g) self-raising flour
1 cup (250ml) pomegranate seeds
2 tablespoons caster sugar
3 teaspoons cornflour
2 tablespoons water

1   Beat butter and sifted icing sugar in small bowl with electric mixer until light and fluffy; transfer to large bowl.
2   Stir sifted flours into butter mixture, in two batches. Knead dough on floured surface until smooth. Divide dough in half; roll each half into 20cm log. Cover with plastic wrap; refrigerate about 45 minutes or until firm.
3   Combine seeds and caster sugar in small saucepan. Blend cornflour with the water in small bowl; add to sugar mixture. Cook, stirring, 2 minutes or until mixture boils and thickens. Cool to room temperature.
4   Preheat oven to 180°C/160°C fan-forced. Grease oven trays.
5   Cut logs into 1cm slices; place 2cm apart on oven trays. Using thumb, make a slight indent, about the size of a 10 cent piece, in top of each cookie. Spoon 1 rounded teaspoon of the pomegranate mixture into each indent. Bake cookies about 12 minutes; cool on trays.

----

prep + cook time 40 minutes
(+ refrigeration and cooling) makes 36

You need 1 large pomegranate (375g) for this recipe. To remove seeds, cut pomegranate in half crossways. Hold one half over a bowl, firmly tap on the skin with a wooden spoon or rolling pin, the seeds should fall out into the bowl.

night before fruit cake

1½ cups (240g) mixed dried fruit
⅓ cup (60g) finely chopped glacé ginger
410g jar fruit mince
175g butter, chopped coarsely
⅔ cup (150g) firmly packed brown sugar
1 teaspoon finely grated lemon rind
2 tablespoons lemon juice
½ cup (125ml) brandy
½ teaspoon bicarbonate of soda
3 eggs, beaten lightly
½ cup (140g) mashed banana
1½ cups (225g) plain flour
½ cup (75g) self-raising flour
½ cup (70g) slivered almonds

1 Combine fruit, ginger, fruit mince, butter, sugar, rind, juice and ⅓ cup of the brandy in medium saucepan; stir over heat until butter is melted and sugar dissolved. Bring to the boil, remove from heat; stir in soda. Transfer to large bowl; cool.
2 Preheat oven to 160°C/140°C fan-forced. Grease 32cm x 22cm rectangular slice pan; line base and two long sides with baking paper, extending paper 5cm above sides.
3 Stir eggs and banana into fruit mixture, then sifted dry ingredients. Spread mixture into pan; sprinkle with nuts.
4 Bake about 55 minutes. Brush hot cake with remaining brandy; cover tightly with foil, cool in pan overnight. Cut cake into 25 squares. Dust cakes with sifted icing sugar to serve, if you like.

----

prep + cook time 1 hour 15 minutes (+ cooling)
serves 25

You need 1 large (230g) overripe banana to get the amount of mashed banana required for this recipe.

gluten-free spicy fruit cake

1¼ cups (200g) sultanas
1 cup (150g) finely chopped seeded dried dates
1 cup (150g) raisins, chopped coarsely
¾ cup (120g) dried currants
1 cup (250g) coarsely chopped glacé apricot
1 cup (250ml) tokay
185g dairy-free margarine
1 cup (220g) firmly packed dark brown sugar
3 eggs
1 cup (120g) almond meal
1½ cups (270g) rice flour
1 teaspoon cream of tartar
½ teaspoon bicarbonate of soda
1 teaspoon ground nutmeg
½ teaspoon ground ginger
½ teaspoon ground cloves

1 Combine fruit and ¾ cup of the tokay in large bowl, cover with plastic wrap; stand overnight.

2 Preheat oven to 120°C/100°C fan-forced. Line deep 22cm-round cake pan with two thicknesses of baking paper, extending paper 5cm above side.

3 Beat margarine and sugar in small bowl with electric mixer until combined; beat in eggs, one at a time. Mix butter mixture into fruit mixture; mix in meal and sifted dry ingredients.

4 Spread mixture into pan; bake about 2½ hours. Brush hot cake with remaining tokay; cover tightly with foil, cool in pan overnight. Serve dusted with sifted pure icing sugar, if you like.

----

prep + cook time 3 hours (+ standing and cooling)
serves 20

Store cake in the refrigerator for up to three months. Cut the cake straight from the fridge, then bring to room temperature before serving.
Tokay is a sweet white fortified wine.

rocky road Christmas trees

75g unsalted butter, chopped coarsely
75g white eating chocolate, chopped coarsely
⅓ cup (75g) caster sugar
⅓ cup (80ml) milk
⅓ cup (50g) plain flour
¼ cup (35g) self-raising flour
1 egg
rocky road
100g toasted marshmallow with coconut,
    cut into 1cm pieces
200g turkish delight, chopped coarsely
½ cup (70g) pistachios, roasted
450g white eating chocolate, melted

1 Preheat oven to 160°C/140°C fan-forced. Grease
8cm x 26cm bar cake pan; line base and sides with
baking paper, extending paper 5cm above long sides.
2 Combine butter, chocolate, sugar and milk in small
saucepan; stir over heat until smooth. Transfer to
medium bowl; cool 10 minutes. Whisk flours then
egg into chocolate mixture. Spread mixture into pan;
bake about 45 minutes, cool in pan.
3 Trim top of cake to make flat; cut 4 x 4.5cm rounds
from cake. Chop cake scraps into 1cm pieces; reserve.
4 Cut four 30cm circles from baking paper. Fold each
circle in half then roll into a cone shape, making sure
the point of cone is closed tight. Staple or tape cone
securely to hold its shape.
5 Make rocky road. Spoon rocky road into cones; press
down firmly to pack tightly. Press one cake round into base
of each cone for a tree stump. Stand each cone upright
in a tall narrow glass. Refrigerate about 1 hour or until set.
6 Remove paper from trees; serve upright on cake base.
rocky road Combine marshmallow, turkish delight, nuts
and chopped cake in large bowl; stir in chocolate.

prep + cook time 1 hour 25 minutes
(+ cooling and refrigeration) **makes** 4

fruit mince friands

6 egg whites
185g unsalted butter, melted
1 teaspoon finely grated orange rind
1 cup (120g) almond meal
1½ cups (240g) icing sugar
½ cup (75g) plain flour
½ cup (150g) fruit mince

1   Preheat oven to 180°C/160°C fan-forced. Grease
12-hole (½-cup/125ml) oval friand pan.
2   Whisk egg whites in medium bowl until frothy. Stir
in butter, rind, meal, then sifted icing sugar and flour.
3   Spoon mixture into pan holes; bake friands 10 minutes.
Remove friands from oven; press a small, 1cm-deep
hole in top of each friand with the end of a wooden
spoon. Spoon fruit mince into holes; bake friands
about 10 minutes.
4   Stand friands in pans 5 minutes before turning,
top-side up, onto wire rack to cool. Serve dusted
with sifted icing sugar.

prep + cook time 35 minutes **makes** 12

Store un-iced cake in the fridge for up to three months. Once iced, the cake can be stored in the fridge for two weeks. Cut and bring to room temperature before serving. We painted a branch of real holly roughly with melted dark chocolate to make the inedible decoration on the cake. Remove cake from fridge, then top with the chocolate decoration.

rich chocolate fruit cake

2 x 425g cans seeded black cherries in syrup
1 cup (150g) raisins, chopped coarsely
¾ cup (120g) finely chopped seeded dried dates
½ cup (80g) sultanas
½ cup (95g) finely chopped seeded prunes
1 cup (200g) dried figs, chopped finely
1 cup (250ml) marsala
1 cup (120g) pecans
185g butter, softened
2 teaspoons finely grated orange rind
1¼ cups (275g) firmly packed dark brown sugar
3 eggs
1¼ cups (185g) plain flour
½ cup (75g) self-raising flour
2 tablespoons cocoa powder
2 teaspoons mixed spice
100g dark eating chocolate, chopped finely
ganache
200g dark eating chocolate, chopped coarsely
½ cup (125ml) cream

1   Drain cherries; reserve ⅓ cup syrup. Quarter cherries. Combine cherries with remaining fruit, ¾ cup of the marsala and reserved cherry syrup in large bowl. Cover; stand overnight.
2   Preheat oven to 150°C/130°C fan-forced. Line deep 22cm-round cake pan with two thicknesses of baking paper, extending paper 5cm above side.
3   Process half the nuts until ground finely; chop the remaining nuts coarsely.
4   Beat butter, rind and sugar in small bowl with electric mixer until combined; beat in eggs, one at a time. Mix butter mixture into fruit mixture; stir in sifted dry ingredients, chocolate and ground and chopped nuts.
5   Spread mixture into pan; bake about 3 hours. Brush hot cake with remaining marsala; cover with foil, cool in pan overnight.
6   Make ganache.
7   Spread cake with ganache; top with chocolate decoration (see tip at top of page). Dust with sifted icing sugar to serve, if you like.
ganache Stir chocolate and cream in small saucepan over low heat until smooth. Refrigerate, stirring occasionally, about 20 minutes or until spreadable.

prep + cook time 3 hours 50 minutes
(+ standing and refrigeration) **serves** 20

white Christmas cake

½ cup (115g) coarsely chopped glacé pineapple
¾ cup (150g) halved red and green glacé cherries
½ cup (115g) coarsely chopped glacé ginger
¼ cup (60g) coarsely chopped glacé figs
¼ cup (60g) coarsely chopped glacé apricots
⅓ cup (55g) mixed peel
1 cup (110g) coarsely chopped walnuts
1 tablespoon marmalade
2 teaspoons finely grated lemon rind
1 tablespoon honey
¼ cup (60ml) sweet sherry
1 teaspoon vanilla extract
250g butter, softened
1 cup (220g) caster sugar
4 eggs
2¼ cups (335g) plain flour
fluffy frosting
1 cup (220g) caster sugar
⅓ cup (80ml) water
2 egg whites

1 Combine fruits, nuts, marmalade, rind, honey, sherry and extract in large bowl; cover, stand overnight.
2 Line deep 20cm-square or deep 22cm-round cake pan with two layers baking paper, bringing paper 5cm above side(s) of pan.
3 Preheat oven to 150°C/130°C fan-forced.
4 Beat butter until smooth; add sugar, beat until combined. Beat in eggs, one at a time. Mix into fruit mixture; stir in sifted flour.
5 Spread mixture into pan; bake about 2½ hours. Cover cake with foil; cool in pan overnight.
6 Make fluffy frosting. Spread cake all over with frosting. Decorate with Christmas ornaments before frosting sets.

fluffy frosting Combine sugar and the water in small saucepan; stir over heat, without boiling, until sugar is dissolved. Boil, uncovered, without stirring, about 5 minutes or until syrup reaches 116°C on a candy thermometer. Syrup should be thick but not coloured. Remove syrup from heat, allow bubbles to subside. Beat egg whites in small bowl with electric mixer until soft peaks form. While motor is operating, add hot syrup in a thin steady stream; beat on high speed about 10 minutes or until mixture is thick.

prep + cook time 3 hours (+ standing and cooling)
serves 20

chocolate fig panforte

¾ cup (110g) plain flour
2 tablespoons cocoa powder
2 teaspoons ground cinnamon
1¾ cups (150g) coarsely chopped semi-dried figs
¼ cup (40g) finely chopped glacé orange
1 cup (160g) blanched almonds, roasted
1 cup (140g) hazelnuts, roasted
1 cup (120g) pecans, roasted
⅓ cup (115g) honey
⅓ cup (75g) caster sugar
⅓ cup (75g) firmly packed brown sugar
2 tablespoons water
100g dark eating chocolate, melted

1 Preheat oven to 150°C/130°C fan-forced. Grease deep 20cm-round cake pan; line base with baking paper.
2 Sift flour, cocoa and cinnamon into large bowl; stir in fruit and nuts. Combine honey, sugars and the water in small saucepan; stir over heat, without boiling, until sugar dissolves. Simmer, uncovered, without stirring, 5 minutes. Pour hot syrup then chocolate into nut mixture; mix well.
3 Press mixture firmly into pan; press a 20cm-round of baking paper on top. Bake 40 minutes; cool in pan.
4 Remove panforte from pan; discard baking paper; wrap in foil. Stand overnight before cutting into thin wedges to serve.

prep + cook time 1 hour 10 minutes (+ standing)
serves 20

boiled fruit cake

5 cups (1kg) mixed dried fruit, chopped coarsely
250g butter, chopped coarsely
1¼ cups (275g) firmly packed brown sugar
1 cup (250ml) sherry
¼ cup (60ml) water
2 teaspoons finely grated orange rind
4 eggs, beaten lightly
1½ cups (225g) plain flour
½ cup (75g) self-raising flour
2 teaspoons mixed spice
½ cup (60g) pecans
¾ cup (105g) macadamias

1   Line deep 22cm-round cake pan with three thicknesses of baking paper, extending paper 5cm above side.
2   Combine fruit, butter, sugar, ¾ cup of the sherry and the water in large saucepan; stir over medium heat until butter is melted and sugar dissolved. Bring to the boil, remove from heat; transfer to large bowl, cool.
3   Preheat oven to 150°C/130°C fan-forced.
4   Stir rind and eggs into fruit mixture then sifted dry ingredients. Spread mixture into pan; top with nuts.
5   Bake cake about 3 hours. Brush hot cake with remaining sherry; cover with foil, cool in pan overnight.

prep + cook time 3½ hours (+ cooling) **serves** 20

This is a rich cake and will keep well. Store it in the fridge in an airtight container.

white chocolate macadamia tartlets

½ cup (110g) firmly packed brown sugar
1 tablespoon cornflour
1 tablespoon golden syrup
25g butter, melted
2 eggs, beaten lightly
2 tablespoons cream
1 teaspoon finely grated lemon rind
1½ cups (210g) macadamias
100g white eating chocolate, melted
pastry
1½ cups (225g) plain flour
⅓ cup (75g) caster sugar
125g cold butter, chopped coarsely
1 egg, beaten lightly
80g white eating chocolate, chopped finely

1 Make pastry.
2 Divide pastry into eight portions. Roll portions, one at a time, between sheets of baking paper, into rectangles large enough to line eight 5cm x 10cm loose-based flan tins. Line tins with pastry; prick bases all over with fork. Cover; refrigerate 30 minutes.
3 Preheat oven to 200°C/180°C fan-forced.
4 Place tins on oven tray; line pastry with baking paper, fill with dried beans or rice. Bake 10 minutes; carefully remove paper and beans. Bake about 5 minutes or until pastry is dry. Cool 15 minutes.
5 Reduce oven temperature to 160°C/140°C fan-forced.
6 Combine sugar and cornflour in medium bowl; stir in syrup, butter, eggs, cream and rind. Place nuts into pastry cases; gently pour sugar mixture over nuts. Bake about 25 minutes; cool. Refrigerate 30 minutes. Remove tartlets from tins; drizzle with chocolate.
pastry Process flour, sugar and butter until crumbly. Add egg; process until combined. Knead chocolate into pastry on floured surface until smooth. Enclose in plastic wrap; refrigerate 30 minutes.

prep + cook time 1 hour 10 minutes
(+ refrigeration and cooling) **makes** 8

These tartlets can be made two days ahead; keep in an airtight container.

This recipe is the famous, delicious Australian Women's Weekly fruit cake; it keeps and cuts superbly.

rich fruit cake

3 cups (500g) sultanas
1½ cups (225g) raisins, chopped coarsely
¾ cup (120g) dried currants
⅔ cup (110g) mixed peel
1 cup (200g) glacé cherries, halved
2 tablespoons marmalade
¾ cup (180ml) dark rum
250g butter, softened
1 teaspoon finely grated orange rind
1 teaspoon finely grated lemon rind
1 cup (220g) firmly packed brown sugar
4 eggs
2 cups (300g) plain flour
½ teaspoon bicarbonate of soda
2 teaspoons mixed spice
2 tablespoons orange marmalade, extra,
    warmed, strained
400g prepared white icing

1   Combine fruit, marmalade and ½ cup of the rum in large bowl, mix well; cover. Stand overnight.
2   Preheat oven to 150°C/130°C fan-forced. Line six deep 10cm-round cake pans with three thicknesses of baking paper, extending paper 5cm above sides.
3   Beat butter, rinds and sugar in small bowl with electric mixer until combined; beat in eggs, one at a time.
4   Mix butter mixture into fruit mixture: stir in sifted dry ingredients. Spread mixture evenly into pans; bake about 1½ hours. Brush hot cakes with remaining rum; cover with foil, cool in pans overnight.
5   Brush tops of cakes with extra marmalade. Roll out prepared icing until 8mm thick. Cut out 6 x 10cm flower shapes from icing; place one shape on top of each cake, smooth surface.

prep + cook time 2 hours 20 minutes
(+ standing and cooling) **makes** 6

Cake mixture can be baked in these well-buttered pans.
12-hole ¾-cup (180ml) texas muffin pan: bake 1¼ hours
14 hole ¾-cup (180ml) petite loaf pan: bake 1 hour
20 hole ½-cup (125ml) oval friand pan: bake 50 minutes

spiced yo-yos with brandy butter

Regular brown sugar can be used instead of dark brown sugar. Unfilled yo-yo's will keep well for about a week in an airtight container. Once filled, the yo-yos will keep in the fridge for a few days.

250g unsalted butter, softened
½ cup (110g) firmly packed dark brown sugar
1½ cups (225g) plain flour
½ cup (75g) cornflour
2 teaspoons ground ginger
1 teaspoon mixed spice
¼ teaspoon ground cloves
brandy butter
100g unsalted butter, softened
⅔ cup (110g) icing sugar
2 tablespoons brandy

1 Preheat oven to 160°C/140°C fan-forced. Grease oven trays; line with baking paper.
2 Beat butter and sugar in small bowl with electric mixer until light and fluffy; stir in sifted dry ingredients, in two batches.
3 Roll rounded teaspoons of mixture into balls; place 3cm apart on trays, flatten slightly using back of a fork. Bake about 15 minutes; cool on trays.
4 Meanwhile, make brandy butter.
5 Sandwich biscuits with brandy butter.
brandy butter Beat butter and sifted icing sugar in small bowl with electric mixer until light and fluffy. Beat in brandy until combined.

prep + cook time 40 minutes (+ cooling) **makes** 32

frozen jaffa slice

Don't worry if the slice cracks after it's removed from the oven, it will contract as it cools down. This slice is very rich; serve in small squares as a petits four.

4 eggs
⅓ cup (75g) firmly packed brown sugar
300g dark eating chocolate, melted
300g tub thick cream (48% fat)
¼ cup (60ml) citrus-flavoured liqueur
3 slices (60g) glacé orange, chopped finely

1 Preheat oven to 180°C/160°C fan-forced. Grease deep 22cm-square cake pan; line base and sides with baking paper.
2 Beat eggs and sugar in small bowl with electric mixer until thick and creamy. Beat in cooled chocolate until combined.
3 Fold in combined cream, liqueur and orange; pour mixture into pan. Place pan in baking dish; pour enough boiling water into dish to come halfway up side of pan. Bake 35 minutes or until slice is barely set; cool slice in pan. Cover; freeze overnight.
4 Remove frozen slice from pan; stand at room temperature 10 minutes. Cut into squares to serve.

prep + cook time 1 hour (+ freezing) **makes** 64

Mince pies will keep well in an airtight container for up to two weeks. Make double the quantity of fruit mince to bottle for gifts.

fig mince pies

150g dried figs, chopped finely
½ cup (65g) dried cranberries
½ cup (75g) raisins, chopped coarsely
¼ cup (40g) mixed peel
¼ cup (55g) finely chopped glacé ginger
¼ cup (60g) finely chopped glacé peach
1 medium apple (150g), grated
½ cup (110g) firmly packed brown sugar
2 tablespoons fig jam
1 teaspoon finely grated orange rind
2 tablespoons orange juice
1 cinnamon stick, halved
1 teaspoon mixed spice
⅓ cup (80ml) brandy
1½ sheets shortcrust pastry, thawed
1 egg white
pastry
2 cups (300g) plain flour
⅓ cup (75g) caster sugar
150g cold butter, chopped coarsely
1 egg, beaten lightly

1 Combine fruit, sugar, jam, rind, juice, spices and brandy in medium bowl. Cover, stand for a week or up to a month; stir mixture every two or three days.
2 Make pastry.
3 Grease two 12-hole (2-tablespoons/40ml) deep flat-based patty pans. Divide pastry in half; roll one portion of dough between sheets of baking paper to 3mm thickness; cut 12 x 7cm rounds from pastry. Repeat with remaining pastry. Press rounds into pan holes; pricks bases all over with fork, refrigerate 30 minutes.
4 Preheat oven to 200°C/180°C fan-forced.
5 Cut whole shortcrust pastry sheet into 16 squares; cut each square into 6 strips. Cut the half pastry sheet into 8 squares; cut each square into 6 strips.
6 Use 6 strips to make a lattice pattern. Cut a 6.5cm round from latticed pastry. Repeat with remaining pastry strips.
7 Discard cinnamon stick from mince, spoon mince into pastry cases; top with lattice pastry rounds. Press edges to seal; brush pastry with egg white. Bake about 20 minutes. Dust with a little sifted icing sugar before serving, if you like.

pastry Blend or process flour, sugar and butter until crumbly. Add egg; process until combined. Knead pastry on floured surface until smooth. Cover; refrigerate 30 minutes.

prep + cook time 1 hour 40 minutes
(+ standing and refrigeration) **makes** 24

brownie bombs

Preheat oven to 180°C/160°C fan-forced. Grease deep 19cm-square cake pan; line base and sides with baking paper. Stir 125g chopped butter and 200g chopped dark chocolate in medium saucepan over low heat until smooth; transfer to large bowl, cool 10 minutes. Stir in ⅔ cup caster sugar, 2 lightly beaten eggs and 1¼ cups sifted plain flour. Spread mixture into pan; bake about 30 minutes. Cool in pan. Cut cake into large pieces; process with ⅓ cup dark rum until mixture comes together. Roll heaped teaspoons of mixture into balls. Freeze for 10 minutes. Melt 200g chopped dark chocolate; dip balls into chocolate to coat. Refrigerate until set. Drizzle with 60g melted white chocolate, decorate with pieces of glacé cherry.

----
prep + cook time 1 hour
(+ cooling and refrigeration) **makes** 50

Christmas muffins

Preheat oven to 200°C/180°C fan-forced. Grease 12-hole (⅓-cup/80ml) muffin pan. Sift 2½ cups self-raising flour into medium bowl; rub in 100g chopped butter. Gently stir in 1 cup caster sugar, 1¼ cups buttermilk and 1 beaten egg. Gently stir in 1 cup mixed coarsely chopped glacé fruit. Spoon mixture into pan holes; bake about 20 minutes. Stand muffins 5 minutes before turning, top-side up, onto wire rack to cool. Roll 250g prepared white icing out to 5mm thick; cut out 12 x 4.5cm stars. Brush tops of muffins with 2 tablespoons warmed, strained apricot jam; top with fondant stars. Dust with sifted icing sugar, if you like.

----
prep + cook time 40 minutes **makes** 12

Christmas cookies

Grease oven trays; line with baking paper. Beat 250g softened butter, ¾ cup caster sugar and 1 egg in small bowl with electric mixer until light and fluffy; transfer to large bowl. Stir in 2¼ cups sifted plain flour. Knead dough on floured surface until smooth; cover, refrigerate 30 minutes. Preheat oven to 180°C/160°C fan-forced. Roll heaped teaspoons of mixture into 15cm log shapes. Twist 2 pieces of dough together, shape into canes and wreaths. Place on trays. Bake about 12 minutes; cool cookies on trays. Sprinkle hot cookies with 2 tablespoons cinnamon sugar.

prep + cook time 30 minutes (+ refrigeration) **makes** 28

fruit nut clusters

Line three 12-hole patty pans with paper patty cases. Stir 150g chopped butter, ½ cup caster sugar and 2 tablespoons honey in small saucepan over low heat until sugar dissolves. Combine 3½ cups cornflakes, ½ cup coarsely chopped dried cranberries, ½ cup roasted flaked almonds, ½ cup coarsely chopped roasted pistachios and ⅓ cup finely chopped glacé peach in large bowl. Stir in butter mixture. Spoon mixture into paper cases; refrigerate until set.

prep + cook time 30 minutes (+ refrigeration) **makes** 36

Classic cakes & puddings

boiled Christmas pudding

1½ cups (250g) raisins
1½ cups (240g) sultanas
1 cup (150g) dried currants
¾ cup (120g) mixed peel
1 teaspoon finely grated
    lemon rind
2 tablespoons lemon juice
2 tablespoons brandy
250g butter, softened
2 cups (440g) firmly packed
    dark brown sugar
5 eggs
1¼ cups (185g) plain flour
½ teaspoon ground nutmeg
½ teaspoon mixed spice
4 cups (280g) stale breadcrumbs

Combine fruit, rind, juice and brandy in large bowl. Cover, stand overnight. Beat butter and sugar in small bowl with electric mixer until combined. Beat in eggs, one at a time. Mix butter mixture into fruit mixture; mix in sifted dry ingredients and breadcrumbs. Tie pudding mixture in pudding cloth; tie tightly with string. Boil pudding 6 hours, replenishing with boiling water as necessary.

prep + cook time 7 hours (+ standing)
serves 16

steamed Christmas pudding

3 cups (450g) chopped mixed
    dried fruit
¾ cup (120g) finely chopped dried
    seedless dates
¾ cup (120g) finely chopped raisins
¾ cup (180ml) water
1 cup (220g) firmly packed
    dark brown sugar
100g butter, chopped coarsely
1 teaspoon bicarbonate of soda
2 eggs, beaten lightly
¾ cup (110g) plain flour
¾ cup (110g) self-raising flour
1 teaspoon mixed spice
½ teaspoon ground cinnamon
2 tablespoons dark rum

Combine fruit, the water, sugar and butter in large saucepan. Stir over heat until sugar dissolves; bring to the boil. Reduce heat; simmer 6 minutes. Stir in soda; cool. Stir in eggs, sifted dry ingredients and rum. Grease 2-litre (8-cup) pudding steamer; spoon mixture into steamer; secure lid. Steam pudding 4 hours, replenishing with boiling water as necessary.

prep + cook time 5 hours (+ cooling)
serves 12

economical boiled fruit cake

2¾ cups (500g) mixed dried fruit
½ cup (125ml) water
1 cup (220g) firmly packed
    dark brown sugar
125g butter, chopped coarsely
1 teaspoon mixed spice
½ teaspoon bicarbonate of soda
½ cup (125ml) sweet sherry
1 egg
1 cup (150g) plain flour
1 cup (150g) self-raising flour
2 tablespoons sweet sherry, extra

Stir fruit, the water, sugar, butter, spice and soda in large saucepan until sugar dissolves; bring to the boil. Reduce heat; simmer, covered, 5 minutes. Stir in sherry; cool. Preheat oven to 160°C/140°C fan-forced. Line deep 20cm-round cake pan. Stir egg and sifted flours into fruit mixture. Spread mixture into pan. Bake cake about 1½ hours. Brush cake with extra sherry; cover cake, cool in pan.

prep + cook time 2 hours (+ cooling)
serves 16

irish pudding cake

This cake can be served hot as a pudding or cold as a cake.

1½ cups (250g) seeded dried
    dates, chopped coarsely
1¼ cups (200g) seeded prunes,
    chopped coarsely
1½ cups (250g) raisins,
    chopped coarsely
1 cup (150g) dried currants
¾ cup (125g) sultanas
1 large apple (200g),
    grated coarsely
1½ cups (375ml) irish whiskey
1¼ cups (275g) firmly packed
    dark brown sugar
185g butter, softened
3 eggs, beaten lightly
½ cup (50g) hazelnut meal
1½ cups (225g) plain flour
1 teaspoon ground nutmeg
½ teaspoon ground ginger
½ teaspoon ground cloves
½ teaspoon bicarbonate of soda

Combine fruit and 1 cup of whiskey in large bowl, cover, stand overnight. Preheat oven to 150°C/130°C fan-forced. Line deep 20cm-round cake pan. Combine remaining whiskey and ½ cup of the sugar in small saucepan. Stir syrup over heat until boiling; cool 20 minutes. Beat butter and remaining sugar in small bowl with electric mixer until combined. Beat in eggs, one at a time. Mix butter mixture into fruit mixture; stir in meal, sifted dry ingredients and ½ cup of the cooled syrup. Spread mixture into pan. Bake about 3 hours. Brush cake with reheated remaining syrup, cover cake; cool in pan.

----
prep + cook time 4 hours
(+ standing and cooling) **serves** 16

celebration fruit cake

3 cups (500g) sultanas
1¾ cups (300g) raisins, halved
1¾ cups (300g) dried dates,
    chopped finely
1 cup (150g) dried currants
⅔ cup (110g) mixed peel
⅔ cup (150g) glacé cherries,
    halved
¼ cup (55g) coarsely chopped
    glacé pineapple
¼ cup (60g) coarsely chopped
    glacé apricots
½ cup (125ml) dark rum
250g butter, softened
1 cup (220g) firmly packed
    dark brown sugar
5 eggs
1½ cups (225g) plain flour
⅓ cup (50g) self-raising flour
1 teaspoon mixed spice
2 tablespoons dark rum, extra

Combine fruit and rum in large bowl; cover, stand overnight. Preheat oven to 150°C/130°C fan-forced. Line deep 22cm-round or deep 20cm-square cake pan. Beat butter and sugar in small bowl with electric mixer until combined. Beat in eggs, one at a time. Mix butter mixture into fruit mixture. Mix in sifted dry ingredients; spread mixture into pan. Bake about 3½ hours. Brush cake with extra rum, cover cake; cool in pan.

----
prep + cook time 4½ hours
(+ standing and cooling) **serves** 20

grand marnier fruit cake

3 cups (500g) sultanas
1½ cups (250g) mixed peel
¾ cup (120g) raisins
¾ cup (120g) seeded dried dates
⅔ cup (140g) seeded prunes
½ cup (125g) glacé apricots
⅔ cup (150g) glacé pineapple
½ cup (70g) slivered almonds
½ cup (60g) coarsely chopped
    walnuts
1 tablespoon finely grated
    orange rind
½ cup (110g) caster sugar
¼ cup (60ml) orange juice
½ cup (125ml) Grand Marnier
250g butter, softened
½ cup (110g) firmly packed
    dark brown sugar
5 eggs
2 cups (300g) plain flour
2 tablespoons Grand Marnier, extra

Combine sultanas and peel in large bowl. Chop remaining fruit the same size as a sultana; add to bowl with nuts and rind. Melt caster sugar in large frying pan, without stirring, until browned. Remove from heat, stir in juice; stir over heat until toffee dissolves. Add liqueur; pour over fruit mixture, cover, stand 10 days, stirring daily. Preheat oven to 150°C/130°C fan-forced. Line deep 20cm-square or deep 22cm-round cake pan. Beat butter and brown sugar in small bowl with electric mixer until combined; beat in eggs, one at a time. Stir butter mixture into fruit mixture, then stir in sifted flour; spread mixture into pan. Bake about 3½ hours. Brush cake with extra liqueur. Cover cake; cool in pan.

----
prep + cook time 4½ hours
(+ standing and cooling) **serves** 20

Christmas decorations

You don't need to spend a heap of money on expensive Christmas decorations...the beautiful pom poms on this page were made using plastic shopping bags. Using minimal decorations can sometimes be more effective than a clutter of heavy traditional ones, especially in warmer climates. Colour co-ordinate with ribbons, flowers, napkins, placemats, etc. A plain white table setting can be co-ordinated with any colour of your choosing, be it traditional red and green, a cool silver and pale blue, or a festive mismatch of bright colours.

Recycled Pom Poms

Cardboard
Plastic shopping bags
Ribbon

Using the template as a guide, cut two identical donut-shaped pieces of cardboard. Cut plastic shopping bags roughly into 2cm-wide lengths (1 bag should make 1 pom pom).
Place the cardboard pieces together. Wind the strips of plastic bag around the cardboard rings (not too tightly, though, as you eventually need to slip your scissors in to cut between the pieces of cardboard). Repeat this, working your way around the ring until all the cardboard is covered once. As you use additional lengths of plastic bag, you don't need to tie them together, just make sure the ends are on the outside, not in the middle. Once the cardboard is covered, insert your scissors between the cardboard pieces (on the outside) and cut the plastic strips around the outside edge (the scissor blades should pass between the two pieces of cardboard as you are cutting.) Gently prise the cardboard pieces apart just enough to be able to pass a strip of plastic bag between the two pieces of cardboard. Pass the strip around all the strands of plastic at the centre, and tie it firmly.
Remove the cardboard rings. Trim any strips that are uneven to give your pom poms a tidy look. Tie each with pretty ribbon and hang on the tree.

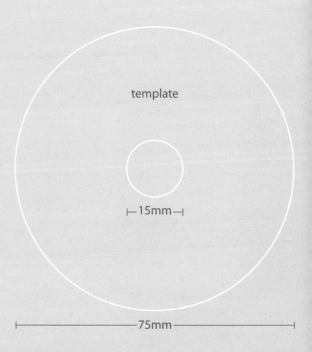

template

├─15mm─┤

├────────75mm────────┤

A Brighter Christmas

Chandelier or lamp
Christmas decorations
Ribbon

Collect your favourite old and new Christmas
decorations. For example; silver stars, silver and
red baubles, glass angels. Thread each with pretty
satin ribbon and attach to a chandelier.

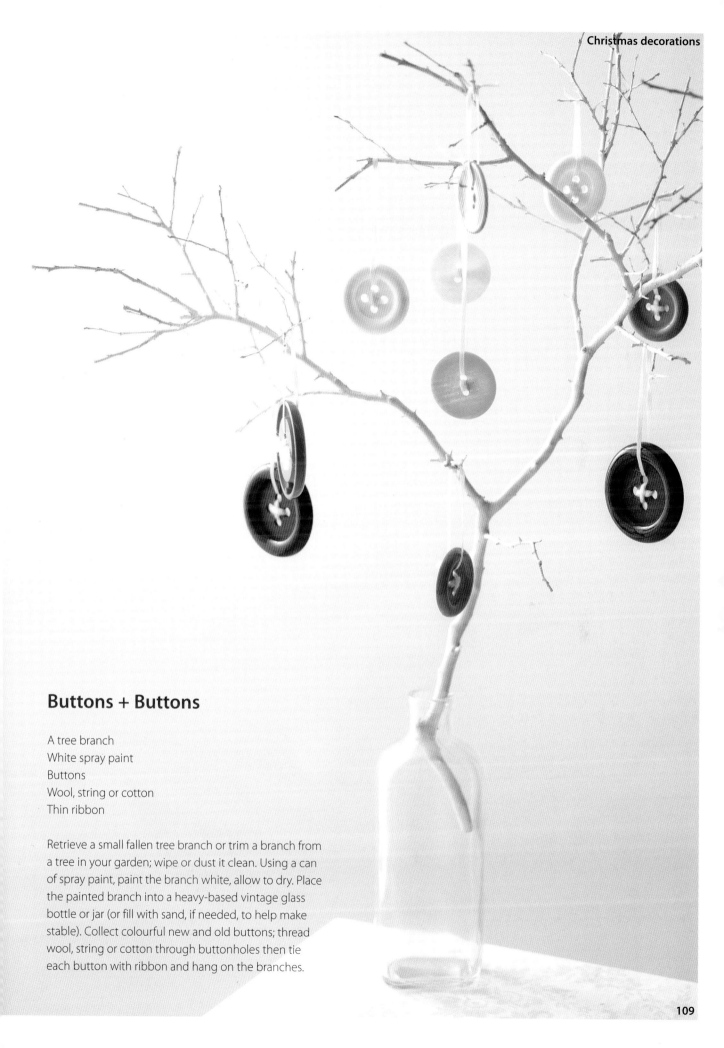

Buttons + Buttons

A tree branch
White spray paint
Buttons
Wool, string or cotton
Thin ribbon

Retrieve a small fallen tree branch or trim a branch from a tree in your garden; wipe or dust it clean. Using a can of spray paint, paint the branch white, allow to dry. Place the painted branch into a heavy-based vintage glass bottle or jar (or fill with sand, if needed, to help make stable). Collect colourful new and old buttons; thread wool, string or cotton through buttonholes then tie each button with ribbon and hang on the branches.

Joyful Christmas

For a pretty feminine Christmas table, choose a pink tablecloth, co-ordinate with pale pink napkins. Add a mix of white and red plates, and a vase of pretty white flowers. Make your own place cards from white cardboard; decorate each with a pink ribbon bow. To finish; add your choice of decorations like white ribbon, pink butterflies and small paper-angel cut outs – all available from craft stores.

A White Christmas

For a very special formal Christmas table setting, start with a white crisp linen tablecloth. Use an eclectic mix of white and silver trimmed plates, vintage silver cutlery tied with white ribbon and pieces of gorgeous vintage lace. Include a large white jug filled with fresh white flowers. Make your own place cards from white cardboard. To finish; decorate each chair with a set of white feathered angel wings (available from children's party shops).

A Green Christmas

For a natural-style Christmas table, cover your tabletop with a plain linen fabric (pages of vintage sheet music make lovely placemats); set with modern oval- or square-shaped plates, plain-woven napkins and wooden cutlery; decorate drinking glasses with pieces of banana leaf (order from greengrocers) or other green leaves secured with string or raffia. Garnish each setting with a large fresh glossy leaf and a small gift (such as chocolates, or fig mince pies, page 100), wrapped in natural calico; tie each with wool or raffia.

Gift Wrapping

Make a story page with postcards or family
photos, and photocopy to make your own
gift wrapping papers, then decorate with
string, buttons or pine tree needles. Recycle or
photocopy vintage maps, books or newspapers
and decorate with string or raffia. Add old
stamps to luggage tags or team with fresh bay
leaves and pieces of vintage sheet music. Use
craft boxes made from recycled paper pulp
(available from craft stores), decorate with a
pretty ribbon and luggage tag to match.

glossary

ALCOHOLIC CIDER fermented from apples. May be sweetened.

BAKING POWDER a raising agent that aerates and lightens cake mixtures.

BASIL, THAI has smallish leaves and a sweet licorice/aniseed taste. Available from many major supermarkets.

BEANS
butter also known as lima beans; a flat, kidney-shaped bean, off-white in colour, with a mealy texture and mild taste.
cannellini small white bean similar to great northern, navy or haricot, each of which can be substituted for the other.

BICARBONATE OF SODA also known as baking or carb soda.

BREAD
french stick bread that's been formed into a long, narrow cylindrical loaf. Is also known as french bread, french loaf or baguette.
lavash flat, unleavened bread used for wrapping or torn and used for dipping.
sourdough so-named because of its very lightly sour taste. A low-risen bread with a dense centre and crisp crust.

BREADCRUMBS
fresh bread, usually white, processed into crumbs.
stale one- or two-day-old bread made into crumbs by blending or processing.

BROCCOLINI a cross between broccoli and chinese kale; milder and sweeter than broccoli. Each long stem is topped by a loose floret that closely resembles broccoli; from floret to stem, broccolini is completely edible.

BUTTER use salted butter; 125g is equal to one stick (4 ounces) of butter.
unsalted often called 'sweet' butter, it simply has no added salt. It's advisable to stick to unsalted butter when it's called for in delicate recipes.

BUTTERMILK originally the term given to the slightly sour liquid left after butter was churned from cream, today it is commercially made similarly to yogurt. Sold alongside all fresh milk products in supermarkets. Despite the implication of its name, it is low in fat.

BUTTERNUT SNAP COOKIE a crunchy biscuit made with golden syrup, oats and coconut.

CAPERS the grey-green buds of a warm climate (usually Mediterranean) shrub, sold either dried and salted or pickled in a vinegar brine. Capers must be rinsed well before using.

CAYENNE PEPPER a long, thin-fleshed, extremely hot red chilli usually sold dried and ground.

CHEESE
blue mould-treated cheeses mottled with blue veining. Varieties include firm and crumbly stilton types to mild, creamy brie-like cheeses.
bocconcini from the diminutive of boccone meaning 'mouthful', this is the term used for a delicate, semi-soft, white cheese. Spoils rapidly so must be kept under refrigeration, in brine, for one or two days at most.
cream commonly known as Philadelphia or Philly, a soft cows-milk cheese. Also available as spreadable light cream cheese, a blend of cottage and cream cheeses.
fetta a crumbly goat- or sheep-milk cheese with a sharp, salty taste.
goats made from goats milk, has an earthy, strong taste; available in both soft and firm textures, in various shapes and sizes, sometimes rolled in ash or herbs.
haloumi a firm, cream-coloured sheep-milk cheese matured in brine; somewhat like a minty, salty fetta in flavour, haloumi can be grilled or fried, briefly, without breaking down. Should be eaten while still warm as it becomes tough and rubbery on cooling.
mascarpone a fresh, unripened, smooth, triple cream cheese with a rich, sweet, slightly acidic taste.

CHERVIL a herb also known as cicily.

CHILLI available in many different types and sizes. Use rubber gloves when seeding and chopping fresh chillies as they can burn your skin.
long red available both fresh and dried; a generic term used for any moderately hot, long (6cm-8cm), thin chilli.
thai also known as 'scuds'; tiny, very hot and bright red in colour.

CHOCOLATE
dark eating also known as semi-sweet or luxury chocolate; made of a high percentage of cocoa liquor and cocoa butter, and a little added sugar.

white eating contains no cocoa solids but derives its sweet flavour from cocoa butter. Very sensitive to heat, so watch carefully if melting.

CHORIZO a sausage of Spanish origin, made of coarsely ground pork and highly seasoned with garlic and chillies.

COCOA POWDER also known as cocoa; dried, unsweetened, roasted then ground cocoa beans (cacao seeds).

CORIANDER also known as pak chee, cilantro or chinese parsley; bright-green leafy herb with a pungent flavour. Both the stems and roots of coriander are also used in cooking; wash well before using. Also available ground or as seeds; these should not be substituted for fresh coriander as the tastes are completely different.

CORNFLOUR also known as cornstarch; used as a thickening agent. Available as 100% maize (corn) and as wheaten cornflour (wheaten has added gluten).

CORNICHONS French for gherkin, a very small variety of cucumber.

COUSCOUS a fine, grain-like cereal product made from semolina flour and water; the dough is sieved then dehydrated to produce tiny even-sized pellets of couscous; it is rehydrated by steaming, or with the addition of a warm liquid, and swells to three or four times its original size.

CRANBERRIES, DRIED have the same slightly sour, succulent flavour as fresh cranberries. Available in supermarkets.

CREAM OF TARTAR the acid ingredient in baking powder; prevents sugar from crystallising in confectionery mixtures, keeps frostings creamy and improves volume when beating egg whites.

CREAM we used fresh cream, also known as pure cream and pouring cream, unless otherwise stated; it has no additives unlike commercially thickened cream. Minimum fat content 35%.
sour a thick commercially-cultured soured cream. Minimum fat content 35%.
thick does not contain any thickening agents and usually has a fat content of around 48% or more.
thickened a whipping cream containing a thickener. Minimum fat content 35%.

crème fraîche mature fermented cream having a slightly tangy, nutty flavour and velvety texture. Minimum fat content 35%.

CUCUMBER, LEBANESE short, slender and thin-skinned. Has tender, edible skin, tiny, yielding seeds, and a sweet, fresh and flavoursome taste.

CUMIN also known as zeera or comino.

CURRANTS, DRIED tiny, almost black raisins so-named after a grape variety that originated in Corinth, Greece.

DAIRY-FREE MARGARINE (dairy-free spread) commercially made margarine, free of dairy products.

EGGPLANT also known as aubergine.
eggplant, baby also known as finger or japanese eggplant.

FENNEL a large vegetable with a white to very pale green-white, firm, crisp bulb. It has a slightly sweet, anise flavour but the leaves have a much stronger taste.

FISH FILLETS, FIRM WHITE any boneless firm white fish fillet – blue eye, bream, swordfish, ling, whiting or sea perch are all good choices. Check for any small pieces of bone in the fillets and use tweezers to remove them.

FLOUR
plain all-purpose flour, made from wheat.
rice very fine flour, made from ground white rice.
self-raising plain flour sifted with baking powder in the proportion of 1 cup flour to 2 teaspoons baking powder.
spelt very similar to wheaten flour, but has a slightly nuttier, sweeter flavour. Available from health-food stores.

FRUIT MINCE also known as mincemeat. A mixture of dried fruits such as raisins, sultanas and candied peel, nuts, spices, apple, brandy or rum. Is used as a filling for cakes, puddings and fruit mince pies.

GINGER also known as green or root ginger; the thick root of a tropical plant.
glacé fresh ginger root preserved in sugar syrup. Crystallised ginger can be substituted if rinsed with warm water and dried before using.
ground also known as powdered ginger; cannot be substituted for fresh ginger.
pickled sold in pieces or sliced, and comes in red and pink varieties packed in a seasoned brine.

GLUCOSE SYRUP also known as liquid glucose, made from wheat or corn starch.

GOLDEN SYRUP a by-product of refined sugarcane; pure maple syrup or honey can be substituted.

GOW GEE WRAPPERS thin pastry rounds made from wheat flour used to wrap around fillings for dumplings; wonton wrappers, spring roll or egg pastry sheets can be substituted.

GREEN MANGO sour and crunchy, green mangoes are just immature fruit. They will keep, wrapped in plastic, in the fridge for up to two weeks.

HARISSA a moroccan sauce or paste made from dried chillies, cumin, garlic, oil and caraway seeds; use as a rub for meats, a sauce or dressing or eat on its own. It is available in supermarkets and Middle-Eastern food shops.

KAFFIR LIME LEAVES also known as bai magrood; looks like two glossy dark green leaves joined end to end, forming a rounded hourglass shape. A strip of fresh lime peel may be substituted for each kaffir lime leaf.

KUMARA Polynesian name of orange-fleshed sweet potato often confused with yam.

LEMON MYRTLE an aromatic plant native to Australia, has a delicious lemon-grass-like flavour. Available ground from specialist food stores and delicatessens.

MAPLE SYRUP a thin syrup distilled from the sap of the maple tree. Maple-flavoured syrup or pancake syrup is not an adequate substitute for the real thing.

MINCE also known as ground meat.

MIRIN a Japanese champagne-coloured cooking wine; made of glutinous rice and alcohol and used for cooking. Should not be confused with sake.

MIXED PEEL candied citrus peel.

MIXED SALAD LEAVES also sold as salad mix, mesclun or gourmet salad mix; a mixture of assorted young lettuce and other green leaves.

MIXED SPICE a blend of ground spices usually consisting of cinnamon, allspice and nutmeg.

MOROCCAN SPICE MIX (seasoning) a spice mix including turmeric, cinnamon and cumin that adds authentic Moroccan flavouring to dishes. Available from most major supermarkets.

MUSHROOMS
enoki clumps of long, spaghetti-like stems with tiny, snowy white caps.
flat large, flat mushrooms with a rich earthy flavour. They are sometimes misnamed field mushrooms, which are wild mushrooms.
swiss brown also known as cremini or roman mushrooms, are light brown mushrooms having a full-bodied flavour. Button mushrooms can be substituted.

MUSTARD
english an extremely hot powdered mustard. A mild variety is also available.
seeds, yellow mainly ground for mustard powder and in prepared mustard preparations. Available from major supermarkets or health-food shops.

OIL
macadamia pressed from ground macadamias. Found in most major supermarkets.
peanut pressed from ground peanuts; has a high smoke point (capacity to handle high heat without burning).
sesame made from roasted, crushed, white sesame seeds; a flavouring rather than a cooking medium.
walnut pressed from ground walnuts. Available from specialist food stores and delicatessens.

ONIONS
green also known as scallion or, incorrectly, shallot; an immature onion picked before the bulb has formed, having a long, bright-green edible stalk.
red also known as spanish, red spanish or bermuda onion; a sweet-flavoured, large, purple-red onion.
shallots also called french shallots, golden shallots or eschalots; small, brown-skinned, elongated members of the onion family. Grows in tight clusters similar to garlic.

PAPAYA also known as pawpaw; large, pear-shaped red-orange tropical fruit.

PAPRIKA ground dried red capsicum (pepper); there are many types available including sweet, smoked and hot.

PARSLEY, FLAT-LEAF also known as continental or italian parsley.

PASTRAMI the word is derived from the Romanian word 'pastra', which means 'to preserve'. A highly seasoned preserved meat usually made from beef.

POMEGRANATE a dark-red, leathery-skinned fruit about the size of an orange filled with hundreds of seeds, each wrapped in an edible lucent-crimson pulp having a tangy sweet-sour flavour.

POTATOES
baby new also known as chats.
kipfler small, finger-shaped potato having a nutty flavour.

PRESERVED LEMON RIND lemons are quartered and preserved in salt and lemon juice or water. To use, remove and discard pulp, squeeze juice from rind, rinse rind well; slice thinly. Sold in jars or singly by delicatessens; once opened, store under refrigeration.

PROSCIUTTO a kind of unsmoked Italian ham; salted, air-cured and aged, it is usually eaten uncooked.

RAISINS dried sweet grapes.

ROCKET also known as arugula, rugula and rucola; a peppery-tasting green leaf. Baby rocket leaves (also known as wild rocket) are smaller and less peppery.

SALAMI cured (air-dried) sausages heavily seasoned with garlic and spices.

SAMBAL OELEK (also ulek or olek) Indonesian in origin; a salty paste made from ground chillies and vinegar.

SAUCES
barbecue a spicy, tomato-based sauce.
fish also called nam pla or nuoc nam; made from pulverised salted fermented anchovies. Has a pungent smell and strong taste, so use sparingly.
soy made from fermented soya beans. Several variations are available in most supermarkets and Asian food stores.
light soy fairly thin in consistency and, while paler than the others, the saltiest tasting; used in dishes in which the natural colour of the ingredients is to be maintained. Not to be confused with salt-reduced or low-sodium soy sauces.
Tabasco brand name of an extremely fiery sauce made from vinegar, thai red chillies and salt.

tomato also known as ketchup or catsup; a flavoured condiment made from tomatoes, vinegar and spices.
worcestershire a dark coloured sauce made from garlic, soy sauce, tamarind, onions, molasses, lime, anchovies, vinegar and seasonings.

SICHUAN PEPPER the peppercorns are reddish-brown in colour, with a strong, pungent aroma and a sharp, tingling and mildly spicy taste. Dry-roast to bring out their full flavour. For sichuan pepper, grind with a mortar and pestle.

SPINACH also known as english spinach and, incorrectly, silver beet.

STAR ANISE a dried star-shaped fruit of a tree native to China. The pods have an astringent aniseed or licorice flavour. Available whole and ground.

SUGAR
caster also known as superfine or finely granulated table sugar.
icing also known as confectioners' sugar or powdered sugar; granulated sugar crushed together with a small amount of added cornflour.
pure icing also known as confectioners' sugar or powdered sugar, but has no added cornflour.
white a coarse, granulated table sugar, also known as crystal sugar.

SULTANAS dried grapes, also known as golden raisins.

TREACLE thick, dark syrup not unlike molasses; a by-product of sugar refining.

TURKISH DELIGHT extremely popular Middle Eastern sweet. Its Turkish name is rahat lokum – meaning 'rest for the throat'. A mixture of syrup and cornflour is boiled with either honey or fruit juice. Most often flavoured with rosewater or peppermint. Available from supermarkets.

TURMERIC, GROUND a spice with a somewhat acrid aroma and pungent flavour. Imparts a golden colour to the dishes of which it's a part.

VANILLA
bean dried long, thin pod from a tropical golden orchid; the tiny black seeds impart a luscious vanilla flavour in baking and desserts. A whole bean can be placed in a sugar container to make the vanilla sugar often called for in recipes.

extract made by pulping chopped vanilla beans with a mixture of alcohol and water. This gives a very strong solution, so only a couple of drops are needed.

VERJUICE unfermented grape juice, with a delicate lemon-vinegar flavour. Available from delicatessens.

VIETNAMESE MINT not a mint at all, but a pungent and peppery narrow-leafed member of the buckwheat family; also known as cambodian mint and laksa leaf.

VINEGAR
balsamic made from the juice of Trebbiano grapes; it is a deep rich brown colour with a sweet and sour flavour. Pungency and quality depend on how long it has been aged.
balsamic, white a clear and lighter version of balsamic vinegar; it has a fresh, sweet clean taste and is now available from most supermarkets.
cider made from fermented apples.
rice wine made from rice wine lees (sediment), salt and alcohol.
sherry made from a blend of wines; left in wooden vats to mature where they develop a rich mellow flavour.
white wine made from white wine.

WATERCRESS one of the cress family, a group of highly perishable peppery greens. Must be used as soon as possible after purchase.

WITLOF also known as endive; cigar-shaped, tightly packed heads with pale, yellow-green tips. Has a delicately bitter flavour. May be cooked or eaten raw.

WOMBOK also known as peking or chinese cabbage or petsai. Elongated in shape with pale green, crinkly leaves, this is the most common cabbage in South-East Asian cooking.

YELLOW PATTY-PAN SQUASH also known as crookneck or custard marrow pumpkins; a round, slightly flat squash being yellow to pale-green in colour and having a scalloped edge. It has a firm white flesh and a distinct flavour.

ZUCCHINI also known as courgette; small, pale- or dark-green, yellow or white vegetable belonging to the squash family. If harvested young, its edible flowers can be baked or fried.

conversion chart

MEASURES

One Australian metric measuring cup holds approximately 250ml; one Australian metric tablespoon holds 20ml; one Australian metric teaspoon holds 5ml.

The difference between one country's measuring cups and another's is within a two- or three-teaspoon variance, and will not affect your cooking results. North America, New Zealand and the United Kingdom use a 15ml tablespoon.

All cup and spoon measurements are level. The most accurate way of measuring dry ingredients is to weigh them. When measuring liquids, use a clear glass or plastic jug with the metric markings.

We use large eggs with an average weight of 60g.

DRY MEASURES

METRIC	IMPERIAL
15g	½oz
30g	1oz
60g	2oz
90g	3oz
125g	4oz (¼lb)
155g	5oz
185g	6oz
220g	7oz
250g	8oz (½lb)
280g	9oz
315g	10oz
345g	11oz
375g	12oz (¾lb)
410g	13oz
440g	14oz
470g	15oz
500g	16oz (1lb)
750g	24oz (1½lb)
1kg	32oz (2lb)

LIQUID MEASURES

METRIC	IMPERIAL
30ml	1 fluid oz
60ml	2 fluid oz
100ml	3 fluid oz
125ml	4 fluid oz
150ml	5 fluid oz (¼ pint/1 gill)
190ml	6 fluid oz
250ml	8 fluid oz
300ml	10 fluid oz (½ pint)
500ml	16 fluid oz
600ml	20 fluid oz (1 pint)
1000ml (1 litre)	1¾ pints

LENGTH MEASURES

METRIC	IMPERIAL
3mm	⅛in
6mm	¼in
1cm	½in
2cm	¾in
2.5cm	1in
5cm	2in
6cm	2½in
8cm	3in
10cm	4in
13cm	5in
15cm	6in
18cm	7in
20cm	8in
23cm	9in
25cm	10in
28cm	11in
30cm	12in (1ft)

OVEN TEMPERATURES

These oven temperatures are only a guide for conventional ovens. For fan-forced ovens, check the manufacturer's manual.

	°C (CELSIUS)	°F (FAHRENHEIT)	GAS MARK
Very slow	120	250	½
Slow	150	275-300	1-2
Moderately slow	160	325	3
Moderate	180	350-375	4-5
Moderately hot	200	400	6
Hot	220	425-450	7-8
Very hot	240	475	9

index

ACP BOOKS
General manager Christine Whiston
Editor-in-chief Susan Tomnay
Creative director & designer Hieu Chi Nguyen
Art director Hannah Blackmore
Senior editor Wendy Bryant
Food director Pamela Clark
Recipe development Cathie Lonnie, Dominic Smith
Food preparation Nicole Jennings, Elizabeth Macri
Sales & rights director Brian Cearnes
Marketing manager Bridget Cody
Senior business analyst Rebecca Varela
Circulation manager Jarna Mclean
Operations manager David Scotto
Production manager Victoria Jefferys

ACP Books are published by ACP Magazines a division of PBL Media Pty Limited
PBL Media, Chief Executive Officer Ian Law
Publishing & sales director, Women's lifestyle Lynette Phillips
Editor-at-Large, Women's lifestyle Pat Ingram
Marketing director, Women's lifestyle Matthew Dominello
Commercial manager, Women's lifestyle Seymour Cohen
Research director, Women's lifestyle Justin Stone

Produced by ACP Books, Sydney.

Published by ACP Books, a division of ACP Magazines Ltd, 54 Park St, Sydney; GPO Box 4088, Sydney, NSW 2001.
phone (02) 9282 8618; fax (02) 9267 9438. acpbooks@acpmagazines.com.au; www.acpbooks.com.au

Printed by Toppan Printing Co, China.

Australia Distributed by Network Services, phone +61 2 9282 8777; fax +61 2 9264 3278;
networkweb@networkservicescompany.com.au

United Kingdom Distributed by Octopus Publishing Group
phone +44(0)207 632 5400; fax +44(0)207 632 5405 www.australian-womens-weekly.com

New Zealand Distributed by Netlink Distribution Company, phone (9) 366 9966; ask@ndc.co.nz
South Africa Distributed by PSD Promotions, phone (27 11) 392 6065/6/7;
fax (27 11) 392 6079/80; orders@psdprom.co.za
Canada Distributed by Publishers Group Canada
phone (800) 663 5714; fax (800) 565 3770; service@raincoast.com

Title: Christmas / food director Pamela Clark.

ISBN 978 1 86396 901 7 (pbk.)

Notes: Includes index.

Subjects: Christmas cookery.

Other Authors/Contributors: Clark, Pamela.

Also Titled: Australian women's weekly.

Dewey Number: 641.5658

© ACP Magazines Ltd 2009
ABN 18 053 273 546
This publication is copyright. No part of it may be reproduced or transmitted in any form
without the written permission of the publishers.

The publishers would like to thank the following for props used in photography:
All Buttons Great and Small, Dedece+, duckegg Blue, Dural Christmas Tree Farm,
Everything Christmas, Ikea, Le Forge, Michael's Shoppe, Papier D'Amour,
That Vintage Shop, The Christmas Shop, Thonet, Venucci, Waterford Wedgwood.

Scanpan cookware is used in the AWW Test Kitchen.

Send recipe enquiries to:
recipeenquiries@acpmagazines.com.au